Professional English in Use

Engineering

Technical English for Professionals

Mark Ibbotson

CAMBRIDGE
UNIVERSITY PRESS

CAMBRIDGE
UNIVERSITY PRESS

University Printing House, Cambridge CB2 8BS, United Kingdom

One Liberty Plaza, 20th Floor, New York, NY 10006, USA

477 Williamstown Road, Port Melbourne, VIC 3207, Australia

4843/24, 2nd Floor, Ansari Road, Daryaganj, Delhi – 110002, India

79 Anson Road, #06–04/06, Singapore 079906

Cambridge University Press is part of the University of Cambridge.

It furthers the University's mission by disseminating knowledge in the pursuit of education, learning and research at the highest international levels of excellence.

www.cambridge.org
Information on this title: www.cambridge.org/9780521734882

First published 2009
Reprinted 2016

Printed in Italy by Rotolito Lombarda S.p.A.

A catalogue record for this publication is available from the British Library

ISBN 978-0-521-73488-2 Edition with answers

Contents

Introduction

Who is this book for?

Professional English in Use Engineering presents around 1,500 of the most important technical words and phrases in English that engineers and engineering technicians need for their work. The vocabulary has been carefully chosen to include:

- terms that are essential in <u>all</u> fields of engineering – for example, all engineers need to discuss dimensions and tolerances, know the names of common materials, and describe how components are fitted and fixed together
- language for discussing and applying key engineering concepts – for example, stress and strain, work and power, and fluid dynamics
- more specific language for mechanical, electrical and civil/structural engineering.

This book is for **professional engineers** who are already familiar with engineering concepts and for **students of engineering**. Language teachers who teach technical English will also find the explanations helpful. The level of English used is **intermediate to upper-intermediate** (Levels **B1** to **B2** in the Common European Framework).

You can use the book on your own for self-study, or with a teacher in the classroom, one-to-one or in groups.

Professional English in Use Engineering is part of the **Professional English in Use** series from Cambridge University Press. More information on this series is available at www.cambridge.org/elt

How is the book organized?

The book has 45 units which are grouped into nine themes. Each theme covers an important area of engineering such as **Materials technology, Static and dynamic principles** and **Mechanisms**. Each unit has two pages. The left-hand page explains key words and phrases and shows you how they are used in context. The right-hand page has exercises which allow you to practise the new language and improve your understanding of how it is used. The **Over to you** activities at the end of each unit (see opposite) are discussion and/or writing activities.

There are 13 **appendices** which provide the professional and student engineer with a reference of English terms used in key engineering activities. For example, language for describing three-dimensional drawings and shapes, the names for the chemical elements and terms for sensing, measuring and regulating devices.

The **answer key** at the back of the book contains answers to all the exercises on the right-hand pages. Most of the exercises have questions with only one correct answer.

The **index** lists all the key words and expressions presented in the book, together with the numbers of the units in which they are presented. It also shows how the terms are pronounced.

The left-hand page

This page presents the key words and phrases for each topic in **bold**. Key vocabulary is introduced using short texts, scripts, diagrams and tables. Many vocabulary items are illustrated. Each unit is divided into sections (usually A and B) and each section has a specific title.

Some sections include **notes** on the key language – for example, explanations of words that have different meanings in technical English and in everyday English, and references to other units where related topics or words are covered in more detail.

The right-hand page

The exercises on the right-hand page allow you to check your understanding of the words and expressions presented on the left-hand page, and to practise using them. There is a wide range of different types of exercise: for example, short texts, gap fills, matching exercises, crosswords and notes to complete.

'Over to you' sections

An important feature of *Professional English in Use Engineering* is the **Over to you** section at the end of each unit. These sections give you the opportunity to use the words and expressions you have just learned, and to relate them to your own work or studies.

How to use the book for self-study

You can work through the book unit by unit, or use the **contents** page at the front of the book to choose specific units that are relevant to you.

Read the texts on the left-hand page and concentrate on the key words and phrases in **bold**. If you find technical terms that are not in bold, look at the index to see if they are explained in another unit. You can also look at the index to help you learn how to pronounce new words. Do the exercises on the right-hand page, then check your answers in the key. If you have made mistakes, go back to the left-hand page and read the texts again. Do the **Over to you** section. Try to use as many new words as possible. It is best to discuss your ideas out loud and to record yourself if you can.

How to use the book in a classroom

Teachers can use *Professional English in Use Engineering* to provide a framework for an 'English for Engineering' course.

The illustrations can often be used as a warm-up activity or as a talking point during the lesson. Sometimes, the left-hand page may be used as the basis for a presentation, by either the teacher or the learners. Learners can do the exercises individually or in small groups. They can then compare answers with other groups or in a whole-class feedback session. The **Over to you** sections can be used as a starting point for role plays, discussions and presentation activities, or adapted to out-of-class projects.

This book is also a perfect complement to *Cambridge English for Engineering* which focuses on communication skills for engineers. More information on this title is available at www.cambridge.org/elt/englishforengineering

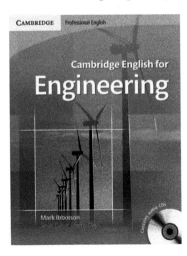

1 Drawings

A Drawing types and scales

In engineering, most design information is shown on **drawings**. Today, drawings are generally not drawn by hand. They are produced on computer, using **CAD (computer-aided design)** systems.

A key factor on a drawing is the **scale** – that is, the size of items on the drawing in relation to their real size. When all the items on a drawing are shown relative to their real size, the drawing is **drawn to scale**, and can be called a **scale drawing**. An example of a scale is 1:10 (**one to ten**). **At 1:10**, an object with a length of 100 mm in real life would measure 10 mm on the drawing.

Most engineering designs consist of **a set of drawings** (a number of related drawings):

- General arrangement (GA) drawings show whole devices or structures, using a **small scale**. This means objects on the drawing are small, relative to their real size (for example, **a 1:100 drawing** of an entire building).

- Detail drawings show parts in detail, using a **large scale**, such as 1:5 or 1:2. Small parts are sometimes shown in a **detail** as **actual size** (1:1), or can be **enlarged** to bigger than actual size (for example, 2:1).

For electrical circuits, and pipe and duct networks, it is helpful to show designs in a simplified form. In this case, **schematic drawings** (often referred to as **schematics**) are used. An everyday example is the map of a train network.

Notes: When written, **drawing** is often abbreviated to **dwg**.
       CAD is pronounced as a word: /kæd/.

B Types of views used on drawings

Technicians are discussing different **views** shown on drawings (looking at components from above, from the side, etc.), as they search for the information they require.

> We need a view from above showing the **general arrangement** of all of the roof panels - a **plan** of the whole area.

> According to this list, there are **elevations** of all four sides of the machine on drawing 28. So one of those should show the front of the machine.

> There should be a **section** through the pipe, showing the valve inside, on drawing 36.

> We need an **exploded view** of the mechanism, showing the components spaced out.

> It's hard to visualize this assembly, based on **two-dimensional** elevations and sections. It would be clearer if we had a **three-dimensional** view, as either an **oblique projection** or an **isometric projection**.

Notes: See Appendix I on page 98 for examples of three-dimensional drawings.

      In non-technical, everyday English, engineering **drawings** are often called **plans**.
      Section is the short form of **cross-section**, and is commonly used in technical contexts.
      Two-dimensional and **three-dimensional** are often shortened to **2D** and **3D**.

1.1 Complete the sentences. Look at A opposite to help you.

1 Enlarged drawings show components larger than their ....actual..........size.......... .
2 For engineering drawings, 1:5 is a commonly used ....scale........... .
3 Whole machines or structures are shown on .....general....arrangement....drawings.
4 Electrical drawings don't usually show sizes. They're shown as ....schematics.... .
5 A ....set.......... of drawings for a large project can consist of hundreds of pages.
6 Most drawings are produced on computers, using ....CAD.......... software.

1.2 Match the descriptions (1–6) with the names of views used on drawings (a–f). Look at B opposite and Appendix I on page 98 to help you.

1 a 2D view of the side of an object   a a plan
2 a 2D view inside an object, as if it is cut through   b a section
3 a 2D view, looking down on top of an object   c an isometric projection
4 a 3D view, showing an assembly taken to pieces   d an oblique projection
5 a 3D view, with the 2D face of the object at the front   e an exploded view
6 a 3D view, with a corner of the object at the front   f an elevation

1.3 Write the full forms, in words, of the abbreviations and shortened terms below. Look at A and B opposite and Appendix I on page 98 to help you.

1 GA   general....arrangement
2 CAD   computer.-.aided....design
3 dwg   drawing
4 3D   three.-.dimensional
5 section cross.-.section
6 1:50   one....to....fifty

1.4 Complete the sentences, taken from conversations about drawings, using the words and abbreviations in the box. Look at A and B opposite and Appendix I on page 98 to help you.

3D	detail	elevation	GA	plan	scale	schematic	section

1 We need a ....section.......... through the bridge, showing the profile of the deck.
2 The only drawing we have is the ....GA........ , which is 1:100, so it obviously doesn't show things in detail.
3 On drawing 12, there's a large ......plan...... of the entire top deck of the ship.
4 This is the ....elevation.... showing the front face of the tower.
5 Modern CAD systems can produce ....3D.............. drawings that look almost as realistic as photographs.
6 We don't need dimensions and positions at this stage. We just need a ......schematic showing how many branches come off the main supply pipe.
7 We don't have a proper drawing. We've just got a rough sketch, which is not to ......scale.......... .
8 The fixings aren't shown on the 1:50 general arrangement. But there's a ....detail...... , at 1:5, on drawing 42.

Over to you

Imagine you are in a meeting at the start of a project. You and your colleagues are about to begin work on the design of a device, installation or structure you're familiar with. What types of drawing will be needed to communicate the design?

2 Design development

Initial design phase

A structural engineer from a firm of consulting engineers has sent an email to a more senior colleague, with an update on a project for a new airport terminal.

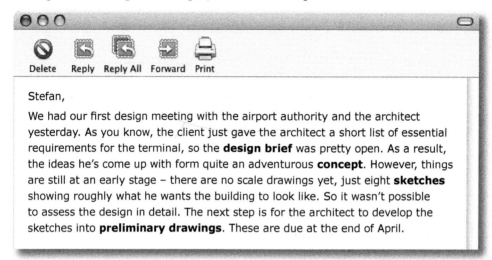

Stefan,

We had our first design meeting with the airport authority and the architect yesterday. As you know, the client just gave the architect a short list of essential requirements for the terminal, so the **design brief** was pretty open. As a result, the ideas he's come up with form quite an adventurous **concept**. However, things are still at an early stage – there are no scale drawings yet, just eight **sketches** showing roughly what he wants the building to look like. So it wasn't possible to assess the design in detail. The next step is for the architect to develop the sketches into **preliminary drawings**. These are due at the end of April.

B Collaborative development

When a design team consists of engineers and consultants from different organizations, the design development process needs to be carefully co-ordinated.

Before the first **draft** (version) of a drawing is sent to members of the team, a decision is made about who needs a copy. Sometimes, a drawing will only be **issued to** certain specialists in the team. Sometimes, it will be **circulated to** all the team members.

After team members have received a drawing, they can **comment on** it, and may ask for the design to be changed. Following these **comments**, the drawing will be **revised** – that is, drawn again with the requested changes made to it. Every drawing is numbered, and each time a drawing is **amended** (revised), the letter next to the drawing number is changed. Therefore drawing 110A, after a **revision**, becomes 110B. When **revision B** is issued, it becomes the **current drawing**, and A is superseded. With each new revision, written **notes** are added to the drawing. These describe the **amendments** that have been made.

When engineers revise drawings during the early stages of the design process, they may have to **go back to the drawing board** (start again), and **redesign** concepts completely. For later revisions, the design should only need to be **refined** slightly.

After a preliminary drawing has been finally **approved** (accepted), a senior engineer can **sign off** (authorize) the drawing as a **working drawing** – that is, one that the production or construction team can **work to**. However, this does not always mean the drawing will be final. Often, working drawings go through more revisions to resolve problems during production.

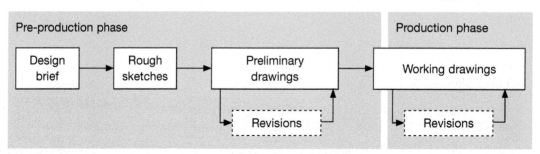

2.1 Find words in A opposite with the following meanings.

1 a description of design objectives → *design brief*
2 a rough, hand-drawn illustration → *sketch*
3 an initial diagram, requiring further development → *preliminary drawing*
4 an overall design idea → *concept*

2.2 Put the words in the box into the table to make groups of verbs with similar meanings. Look at B opposite to help you.

amend	circulate	redesign	revise	supersede
approve	issue	refine	sign off	

1	2	3	4
change improve *amend* *redesign* *revise* *refine*	send out distribute *issue* *circulate*	accept agree *sign off* *aprove*	replace *supersede*

2.3 Choose the correct words from the brackets to complete the sentences about drawings. Look at B opposite to help you.

1 Has the drawing been revised, or is this the first (*draft*/refine)?
2 This has been superseded. It's not the (*current*/preliminary) drawing.
3 Has this drawing been signed off? Can they (circulate/*work*) to it in the factory?
4 I still need to (*comment*/note) on the latest set of drawings.
5 Construction can't start until the first (current/*working*) drawings have been issued.

2.4 Complete the email using the correct forms of the words in the box. Look at B opposite to help you. The first one has been done for you.

amendment	current	draft	issue	note	revision	supersede	work

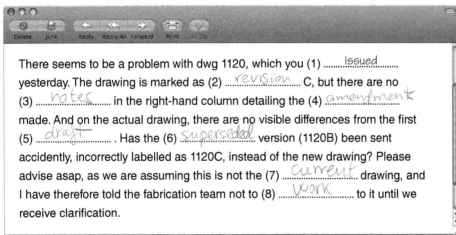

There seems to be a problem with dwg 1120, which you (1) ......*issued*...... yesterday. The drawing is marked as (2) ...*revision*... C, but there are no (3) ...*notes*... in the right-hand column detailing the (4) *amendment* made. And on the actual drawing, there are no visible differences from the first (5) ...*draft*... . Has the (6) *superseded* version (1120B) been sent accidently, incorrectly labelled as 1120C, instead of the new drawing? Please advise asap, as we are assuming this is not the (7) ...*current*... drawing, and I have therefore told the fabrication team not to (8) ...*work*... to it until we receive clarification.

Over to you

Think about design development on a project you have worked on, or on a type of project you know about. Describe the key stages from the design brief to the issue and ongoing revision of working drawings. Say how designers, consultants and production teams are involved at each stage of the process, and explain what procedures are used.

3 Design solutions

A Design objectives

The web page below is from a manufacturing company's intranet.

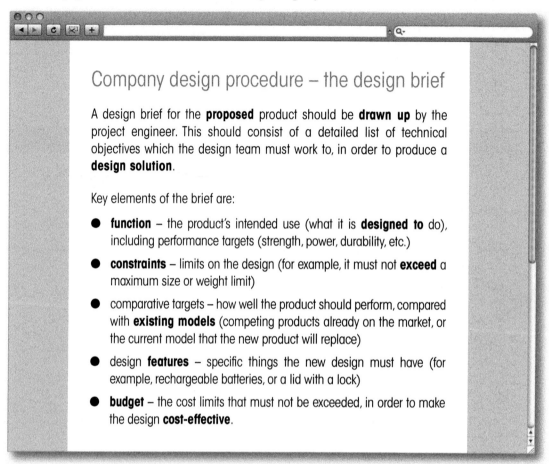

Company design procedure – the design brief

A design brief for the **proposed** product should be **drawn up** by the project engineer. This should consist of a detailed list of technical objectives which the design team must work to, in order to produce a **design solution**.

Key elements of the brief are:

- **function** – the product's intended use (what it is **designed to** do), including performance targets (strength, power, durability, etc.)
- **constraints** – limits on the design (for example, it must not **exceed** a maximum size or weight limit)
- comparative targets – how well the product should perform, compared with **existing models** (competing products already on the market, or the current model that the new product will replace)
- design **features** – specific things the new design must have (for example, rechargeable batteries, or a lid with a lock)
- **budget** – the cost limits that must not be exceeded, in order to make the design **cost-effective**.

B Design calculations

Design information is shown on drawings, and written in **specifications** – documents which describe the materials, sizes and technical requirements of components. In order to **specify** this detailed information, an engineer must **evaluate** – that is, identify and calculate – the **loads** (forces) that key components will have to carry. To do this, the engineer needs to **determine** (identify) the different loads, then **quantify** them – that is, calculate them in number form. Usually, each load is quantified based on a **worst-case scenario** – in other words, the engineer will **allow for** the maximum load, such as an aircraft making a very hard landing, or a bridge being hit by extremely high winds.

After maximum loads have been quantified, an engineer will apply a **factor of safety**. This is an extra margin to make the component strong enough to carry loads that are higher than the worst-case scenario. For example, a factor of 1.5 increases the load a component can carry by 50%. After this has been **factored in**, the engineer will then **size** the components – that is, calculate their required size.

Engineers are sometimes criticized because they **overdesign** things (add excessive factors of safety), which increases costs. However, according to **Murphy's Law**, 'Anything that can go wrong, will.' This suggests that **belt and braces** – an expression often used in engineering, based on the safest method of holding up trousers – is a sensible approach.

3.1 Complete the sentences from technical conversations using the words in the box. Look at A opposite to help you.

budget	cost-effective	exceed	feature	proposed
constraint	designed	existing	function	

1 Of course, money is limited. Cost limitations are always a _Constraint_. But some finance is available. A _budget_ has been allocated for the preliminary design phase – a total of $35,000. But we mustn't _exceed_ that amount.

2 Obviously, if we have to spend €80 on components for each appliance, and the appliances are sold for €70, that's not a _cost-effective_ design solution.

3 The _function_ of this detector is to locate underground cables by giving audio feedback. Since it's _designed_ to be used in noisy environments, the earphone is an important _feature_ .

4 Are these already on the market – are they _existing_ products? Or are we talking about _proposed_ products that are still under development?

3.2 Choose the correct words from the brackets to complete the sentences. Look at B opposite to help you.

1 The types of loads that will be encountered must be (designed / _determined_).
2 Maximum loads are based on predicted (specifications / _worst-case scenarios_).
3 On top of maximum loads, additional safety margins are (_factored in_ / sized).
4 For cost reasons, components shouldn't be (_overdesigned_ / quantified).
5 The practice of overdesigning components can be described as the (_belt and braces_ / factor of safety) approach.
6 (Quantifying / _Sizing_) components means calculating their dimensions.

3.3 Replace the underlined words and expressions with alternative words and expressions from A and B opposite.

factor in for ~~allow for~~

Most engineering designs (1) <u>make provision for</u> excessive or abnormal operating conditions. The critical question is, how much of a (2) <u>percentage of extra size or capacity</u> _factor of safety_ should be applied without (3) <u>adding too much of a margin</u>? To (4) <u>calculate an amount</u> _overdesigning_ _quantify_ <u>for</u> this figure, it is critical to assess the consequences of a technical failure. Where the stakes are high, in applications such as aviation, designing for (5) <u>the most extreme</u> _the worst-case scenario_ <u>situations</u> is clearly critical on safety grounds. On the face of it, the result of this may seem costly. But where the human implications and expense of failure are serious, a high level of expenditure aimed at accident prevention can be considered (6) <u>financially viable</u>.

cost-effective

Over to you

Think about overdesign in a field of engineering you are familiar with. How easy or difficult is it to predict and quantify loads? How serious are the consequences (human and financial) of technical failures? As a result, how high are typical factors of safety?

Horizontal and vertical measurements

A   Linear dimensions

The web page shows the key **dimensions** of the Airbus A380 in metres, and the explanations below it describe how they are **measured**. In the explanations, the word **plane** means an imaginary surface (not an aeroplane). On drawings, planes are shown as lines that indicate where dimensions are measured **from** and **to**, and are positioned to **strike** (touch) the **faces** (edges or surfaces) of components. Often, they are either **horizontal planes** or **vertical planes**.

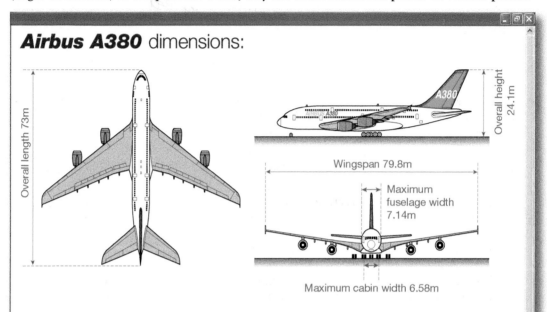

Airbus A380 dimensions:

Overall length 73m

Overall height 24.1m

Wingspan 79.8m

Maximum fuselage width 7.14m

Maximum cabin width 6.58m

Overall length is a measurement of how long the aircraft is in total. The **measurement** is **taken** between the two points that are furthest apart (the front and rear **extremities**), **along the length** of the aircraft. The length is **measured along** a horizontal plane. It is the distance between a vertical plane striking the front of the nose, and a vertical plane striking the rear of the tail.

Wingspan is the total distance **spanned** by both wings. The **span** is measured as a straight line between the two wingtips.

Overall **height** measures how tall the aircraft is. The dimension is **measured vertically** between the underside of the wheels and a horizontal plane striking the top of the tail.

Maximum fuselage **width** is the **external width** of the aircraft's body – how wide it is, **measured horizontally** between vertical planes striking the outside faces of the fuselage.

Maximum cabin width states the maximum **internal** width, measured between the inside faces of the fuselage. The measurement is equivalent to the external width, less the **thickness** of the fuselage at each side of the aircraft.

Notes: When written, the words **dimension** and **dimensions** are often abbreviated to **dim** and **dims**.
Span is also used to describe the distance(s) crossed by a bridge, between its supports. If a bridge has a support at its centre (as well as at each end), then it has two **spans**.

B   Level and plumb

If a surface is described as being **level**, this means it is both horizontal and **flat** (smooth). However, a surface which is flat is not necessarily horizontal. A flat surface may be vertical, or **inclined** (sloping **at an angle to** the horizontal or vertical plane).

Faces that are vertical, such as those of the walls of buildings, are described by engineers as being **plumb**. Structures that are slightly **inclined from** vertical are said to be **out of plumb**.

4.1 Complete the key dimensions of the Millau Viaduct in France, using the words in the box. Look at A opposite to help you.

height	overall	thickness	span	width

(1) _overall_ length: 2,460 m

(2) Maximum _span_ between supports: 342 m

(3) _height_ of tallest support (ground to deck): 245 m

(4) _width_ of deck: 32 m

(5) _thickness_ of deck: 4.2 m

4.2 Decide whether the sentences about the viaduct are true or false, and correct the false sentences. Look at A and B opposite to help you.

1 The height of the towers is measured horizontally. *vertically*

2 The overall span is measured along the width of the bridge. *length*

3 The tops of the towers are at different levels, so a horizontal plane striking the top of one tower will not strike the tops of all the others. *t*

4 The highest point of the structure is the top extremity of the highest tower. *t*

5 The thickness of each tower decreases towards the top, so the faces of the towers are *out of* plumb.

6 The greatest thickness of each tower is its internal thickness at its base. *external*

4.3 Circle the correct words to complete the text about extra-high voltage (EHV) power lines. Look at A and B opposite to help you. The first one has been done for you.

On EHV transmission lines, cables – called conductors – (1) *incline /* **span** between pylons, which are described as supports. The conductors are suspended from the supports by rods, called insulators. On straight sections of line, the insulators are (2) *level /* **plumb**, hanging vertically from the supports. At supports where the direction of the line changes, pairs of insulators are used. In this situation, the insulators are (3) **inclined** */ striking* from the vertical plane, as they are pulled (4) *plumb /* **out of plumb** by the conductors pulling in different directions.

The higher the voltage being transmitted by the line, the greater the required distance between the conductor and the support, in order to provide effective insulation. The (5) **length** */ width* of insulators therefore varies, depending on the voltage. Higher voltages also mean that conductors must be located at a greater minimum (6) **height** */ thickness* above the ground, for safety. This distance is measured between the ground and the lowest point of the cable.

4.4 Read the text below. Can you answer the questions?

On long suspension bridges, when the distance between the vertical centres of the towers at either side of the bridge is measured horizontally, the distance between the tops of the two towers will be several millimetres longer than the distance between their bases. Does this mean the towers are out of plumb? Why is there a difference?

curvature of earth

Over to you

Think of a product with a fairly simple shape. What dimensions would need to be specified on a drawing in order to allow the product to be manufactured?

5 Locating and setting out

A Centrelines and offsets

The drawing below shows the position of some holes for bolts. The distances between the holes can be shown as **running dimensions** or as **chain dimensions**. In both cases, the **centreline** (**CL**) – a line through the centre of the hole – is **marked** (drawn), and the distances between the centrelines are given. Distances between centrelines are called **centre-to-centre** (**c/c**) dimensions. The holes below are **at 100 mm centres**.

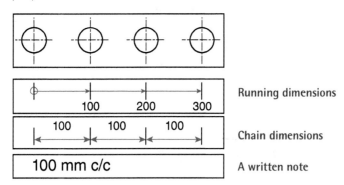

Running dimensions

Chain dimensions

A written note

Centrelines are often used as **reference points**. These can be measured from, in order to **locate** – that is, give the position of – points on components. The measurements are **offset from** the centreline – each is at a certain distance from it, and the **offsets** are measured **at a right-angle to** the centreline (at 90 degrees to it).

Note: We can say *at a right-angle* to X, at *90 degrees* to X, or at *right-angles* to X.

B Grids

In large designs, notably those of structures, **grids** are used for horizontal positioning. The **gridlines** have numbers and letters. All numbered gridlines are **parallel with** one another – that is, they are straight, and are regular distances apart. Lettered lines also **run parallel with** one another, and are **perpendicular to** (at a right-angle to) the numbered lines.

The plan below shows part of the floor of an office building. The **perpendicular** gridlines **intersect at** (cross at) the centres of columns. An opening (hole) in the floor is shown using **coordinate dimensions**. These allow the site engineer to **set out** (mark the position of) the opening by **squaring off** the gridlines – marking lines that run at a right-angle to them – and then measuring along these lines using a **tape measure**.

A **theodolite** – an optical device used for measuring angles – can be used to square off gridlines accurately. To **double-check** dimensions – that is, carry out an extra check – **diagonal measurements** can be used, as in the engineer's sketch below. The length of **diagonals** can be calculated using Pythagoras's Theorem.

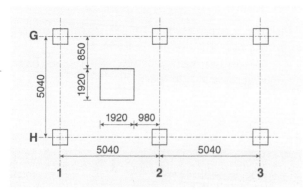

Drawing

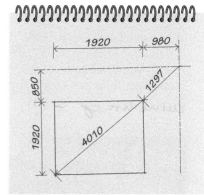

Site engineer's sketch

5.1 Look at the sentences about the design of a ship. Replace the underlined words and expressions with alternative words and expressions from A opposite.

1 The handrail is fixed by 115 brackets, which are <u>175 mm apart, between their centres</u>. *centres*

2 The dimensions are measured from the <u>line down the middle</u> of the ship. *Centreline*

3 How far is the widest point of the ship <u>located away</u> from the centreline? *offset*

4 Are the adjacent lengths of handrail <u>at 90 degrees</u> to each other? *perpendicular, at a right angle*

5 These dimensions allow you to <u>establish the position of</u> the hole. *locate*

5.2 Look at the extracts from technical discussions on a construction site. Complete the sentences using the words in the box. Look at B opposite to help you.

| gridline   intersect   parallel   perpendicular   set out   square off |

1 According to this drawing, ...*gridline*...... 8 runs along the external wall of the structure.

2 The positions were marked accurately – they were ......*set out*...... by our site engineer.

3 The external wall runs along gridline 1, and the internal corridor wall runs along gridline 2, so the walls are ......*parallel*...... with each other.

4 I've marked a cross on the concrete floor, showing where the two gridlines ......*intersect*......

5 We need to show the position of the corner of the staircase with coordinate dimensions. There should be two ......*perpendicular*...... dimensions, taken from two gridlines.

6 We'll use the theodolite to ......*square off*...... the gridline and mark a ninety-degree offset.

5.3 Match the two parts of the sentences to complete the extract from a training manual. Look at A and B opposite to help you.

In civil engineering, the following precautions can help to prevent costly setting-out mistakes.

(1) Always use a steel tape measure (never a plastic one) *b*
(2) Check that both diagonals of rectangular shapes are equal *a*
(3) Measure dimensions in two directions, from parallel gridlines, *d*
(4) Add up chain dimensions to give running dimensions *c*

a   to check that corners are right-angles.

c   to prevent slight errors being multiplied.

b   to ensure it does not stretch under tension.

d   to double-check your measurements.

Over to you

Choose a nearby object, or part of a building. Describe it, using language from A and B opposite. (You could also give approximate measurements.) Then imagine you are designing the object or the part of the building. What dimensions and lines will be needed on the drawings in order to locate its features?

6 Dimensions of circles

A Key dimensions of circles

An engineer is giving a training course to a group of technical sales staff who work for a tyre manufacturer. During the talk, she mentions a number of dimensions relating to circles.

'Obviously, the outside edge of a tyre forms a **circle**, as you can see in this simple diagram. The **outer circle** in the diagram is the outside of the tyre, and the **inner circle** – the circle with the smaller **diameter** – represents both the inside of the tyre and the outside of the wheel. And, clearly, the inner circle is right in the middle of the outer circle – it's exactly in the **centre**. So because it's **central**, that means the inside and outside of the tyre form **concentric circles**. And as the tyre is **circular**, simple geometry tells us that measurements of the **radius**, taken from the centre of the circle to different points on its edge – points on the **circumference** – are equal. All the **radii** are the same. In other words, the tyre has a **constant radius**.'

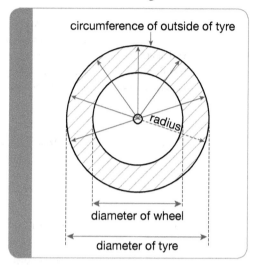

circumference of outside of tyre

radius

diameter of wheel

diameter of tyre

'But when a tyre is fitted to a vehicle, it's compressed against the road surface. That means its geometry changes. So while the wheel – the inner circle – obviously remains **round**, the circumference of the tyre – the outer circle – changes shape. It **deforms**. Before **deformation**, this part of the tyre forms an **arc** of the circle, between points A and B. So, as you can see in this diagram, it's not a straight line – it's a **curved** line. But after deformation, it's no longer a **curve**. The tyre becomes **deformed** between points A and B. It becomes a **chord** of the same circle, forming a <u>straight</u> line between A and B. However, the length of a chord and the length of an arc, between the same two points on a circle, are different. So the design of the tyre has to allow for this change in shape – from a **rounded** edge to a straight edge.'

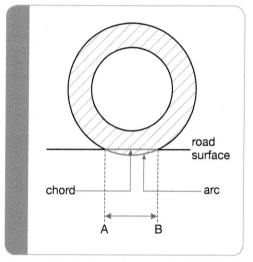

road surface

chord

arc

A   B

Note: See Appendix II on page 99 for more on shapes.

B Pipe dimensions

Specific terms are used to describe the circular dimensions of pipes. The width of the inside of a pipe is called the **inside diameter** (**ID**). It can also be called the **bore**. The outside width is called the **outside diameter** (**OD**). When pipes are laid horizontally, the top of the outside of the pipe is called the **crown**, and the bottom of the inside of the pipe is called the **invert**.

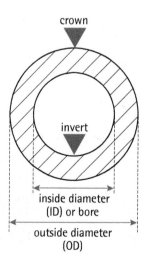

crown

invert

inside diameter (ID) or bore

outside diameter (OD)

6.1 Complete the notes, made by a salesperson attending the engineer's talk, using the words in the box. Look at A opposite to help you.

arc	circular	constant	deformed	radius
chord	circumference	curved	diameter	

Before tyres are fitted to vehicles:
- shape is round — outside edge is perfectly (1) *circular*
- distance from centre of wheel to edge of tyre = (2) *radius*
- total distance across tyre = 2 × radius = (3) *diameter* of tyre
- all measurements from centre to points around tyre's (4) *circumference* are equal — tyre has (5) *constant* radius
- bottom of tyre is (6) *arc* of a circle

When fitted to vehicle, bottom of tyre is compressed and (7) *deformed* — changes from (8) *curved* line to straight line. Straight line is (9) *chord* of a circle.

6.2 Find words and expressions in B opposite with the following meanings. One question has two possible answers.

1 the highest point of a horizontal pipe → *crown*
2 the lowest point of the inside of a horizontal pipe → *invert*
3 the maximum overall external width of a pipe → *outside diameter*
4 the maximum internal width between the pipe walls → *bore*

6.3 Change one word in each of the sentences below to correct them. Look at A and B opposite to help you.

1 The distance travelled by the vehicle each time its wheels turn completely is equal to the ~~radius~~ *circumference* of one of its tyres.
2 The ~~diameter~~ *radius* of the tyre is measured from the centre of the wheel to the outside edge of the tyre.

3 The radius of the curve in the motorway is constant, so the edges of the road follow ~~chords~~ *arcs* of a circle.
4 The curve in the motorway has a constant radius, so the inside and outside edges of the road are arcs of two ~~deformed~~ *concentric* circles that have the same centre.
5 The ~~invert~~ *crown* is on the circumference of the external face of the pipe, and therefore cannot be in contact with the liquid flowing inside the pipe.
6 The thickness of the wall at the bottom of the pipe, plus the distance between the invert and the crown of the pipe, is equal to the ~~inside~~ *outside* diameter of the pipe.

Over to you

- Choose an object which has circular and/or curved shapes. Describe it using language from A opposite. (You could also give approximate measurements.)
- Imagine you are designing the object. What measurements and lines will be needed to define its circular/curved features?

7 Dimensional accuracy

A Precision and tolerance

It is impossible to produce components with dimensions that are absolutely **precise**, with sizes <u>exactly</u> the same as those specified in a design. This is because all production processes are **imprecise** to a certain extent. Therefore, the sizes of several components produced from the same design will **vary** (differ). Although the **variation** may only be a few hundredths of a millimetre, sizes will not be 100% **accurate** (exact) compared with the design.

Because engineers know that **accuracy** cannot be perfect, in designs they often specify **tolerances** – that is, acceptable variations in **precision**. Instead of giving one precise size, a tolerance specifies a **range** of acceptable sizes – an allowed amount of variation. This is often given as a **deviation** (difference) from a precise size.

The drawing below shows a shaft with a specified diameter of 88 mm, **plus or minus** (±) 0.05 mm. This means the diameter may **deviate** 0.05 mm either side of this size. Therefore, diameters of 87.95 mm and 88.05 mm, which are slightly **inaccurate**, are still **permissible** (allowed), as they are **within tolerance**. However, diameters of 87.94 mm or 88.06 mm are not permissible – they are **outside tolerance**.

shaft Ø 88 mm ± 0.05

When the permissible deviation in size is very small, we say it is a **tight tolerance** (or a **close tolerance**). A large permissible deviation is a **loose tolerance**. For example:

- Machining a metal component to a tolerance of ±0.1 mm is relatively easy to do, so this tolerance is loose. But a tolerance of just ±0.01 mm is a tight tolerance in metalworking.

- In a concrete structure, ±10 mm is a loose tolerance. But ±1 mm is tight, because it is difficult to place wet concrete accurately.

B Fit

When one component goes through another, such as a shaft or a bolt going through a hole, the two must **fit together** – their sizes and shapes must match. The key question is, how tightly (or loosely) should they fit together? There are two main types of **fit**:

- A **clearance fit** allows a component to slide or turn freely, by leaving **clearance** (a gap) between itself and the sides of the hole. This distance must be quite precise. If there is **insufficient clearance** – if the gap is too small – the component will fit too tightly. As a result, the component will **bind** – it will not be able to slide or turn freely. In other words, there will not be enough **play**. However, if there is too much clearance, there will be **too much play** and the component will be able to move too much.

- An **interference fit** is a very tight fit which does not allow a component to move freely inside a hole. This type of fit can be achieved by forcing the component into the hole. Alternatively, the metal around the hole can be heated so that it **expands** (increases in size due to heat). After sufficient **expansion**, the component is placed in the hole. The metal then cools and **contracts** (decreases in size due to cooling). The **contraction** results in a tight fit. An example of an interference fit is a train wheel fitted on an axle.

7.1 Find words and expressions in A opposite with similar meanings to the words and expressions below (1–10). Sometimes there is more than one possible answer. The first one has been done for you.

1 allowed   *permissible*
2 exact *accurate*
3 differ *vary*
4 exactness *accuracy*
5 not exact *deviate*

6 deviation between maximum and minimum *tolerance*
7 an acceptable deviation *within tolerance*
8 an unacceptable deviation *outside tolerance*
9 little deviation allowed *tight*
10 large deviation allowed *loose*

7.2 Match the related sentences. Look at B opposite to help you.

1 It'll bind.
2 It'll contract.
3 It'll expand.
4 There'll be too much play.
5 It needs a clearance fit.
6 It needs an interference fit.

a The bolt will have to turn in the hole.
b The bolt won't be able to turn freely enough in the hole.
c The bolt won't fit tightly enough in the hole.
d The wheel will have to fit very tightly on the axle.
e The hole will widen with the high temperature.
f The shaft will shorten and narrow slightly as it cools.

7.3 Complete the article about engine blueprinting using the words in the box. Look at A and B opposite to help you.

clearances	minus	plus	range	variation
fit	permissible	precise	tolerances	within

Blueprinting for performance

The advantage of racing in a kart class with a standard engine spec seems obvious – everyone has the same power, so it's driving talent that makes the difference. But things aren't quite that simple. No two standard engines are identical. There will always be a slight (1) *variation* in the size of engine parts, since they are manufactured, not to perfectly (2) *precise* dimensions, but to specified (3) *tolerances*. Although these differences may only be (4) *plus* or (5) *minus* a few hundredths of a millimetre, they will nevertheless result in a slight performance gap between any two engines.

One way round this problem (if you have the cash) is to have your engine blueprinted. The process is perfectly legal, as the sizes of all parts remain (6) *within* the tolerances that are (7) *permissible* for the standard engine specification. However, by carefully matching pairs or groups of parts that are all in either the lower or upper half of the tolerance (8) *range*, a blueprinted engine is built to (9) *fit* together very precisely, thanks to almost perfect (10) *clearance* between moving parts.

Over to you

Think of a type of product or structure you're familiar with. Imagine you're designing it, and are discussing the tolerances required for different components. Say what tolerances are permissible, both for production (not too tight due to cost), and for quality (not too loose). Say which parts require the tightest tolerances, and explain why.

8 Numbers and calculations

A Decimals and fractions

A manufacturer is thinking about giving both **metric** measurements (for example, millimetres) and **imperial** measurements (for example, inches) in its product specifications. One of the company's engineers is giving his opinion on the idea in a meeting.

'One problem is, when you convert from metric to imperial you no longer have **whole numbers** – you get long **decimal numbers**. For example, one millimetre is **nought point nought three nine three seven** inches as a **decimal**. So to be manageable, decimals have to be **rounded up** or **down**. You'd probably round up that number **to two decimal places**, to give you **zero point zero four**. Now, you might say the difference is **negligible** – it's so small it's not going to affect anything. But even if it's just a tiny **fraction** of a unit – **one hundredth of** an inch (1/100), or **one thousandth of** an inch (1/1000) – and those numbers are then used in calculations, the **rounding error** can very quickly add up to give bigger inaccuracies.'

Note: See Appendix III on page 100 for a list of metric and imperial units.

$1 \text{ mm} = 0.03937 \text{ inches} \approx 0.04 \text{ inches}$

B Addition, subtraction, multiplication and division

During a TV programme about garden design, the presenter is explaining the calculations required to make a large setsquare which can be used for setting out.

> To make one of these, you need to use Pythagoras's Theorem. So, a quick geometry lesson. Measure a length of timber for one of the sides adjacent to the right-angle. I've made this 3 feet long. Then **square** that number – 3 **multiplied by** 3 **equals** 9. Then do the same with the other side adjacent to the right-angle. I've made this one 4 feet long. Work out **the square of** that. So, 4 **times** 4 is 16. Then work out **the sum of** those two numbers – so if I **add** 16 to 9 ... 16 **plus** 9 is 25. Then, calculate **the square root of** that. The square root of 25 is 5. That means the longest side – the hypotenuse – needs to be 5 feet long. And it doesn't matter what length you make the two adjacent sides – if the square of the hypotenuse is **equal to** the square of each of the adjacent sides, **added together**, you'll have a perfect right-angle.

A large setsquare for setting out

> Now you can also start by making the hypotenuse, square the length of that, then make one of the other sides, square the length of that, and then **subtract** one **from** the other. For this example, that would be 25 **minus** 16. So, 25 **less** 16 is 9. And the square root of 9 is 3, which gives me the remaining side. Alternatively, you can make both the adjacent sides **equal** – make them the same length. So, take the square of the hypotenuse, which is 25, **divide** that **by** 2, which is 12.5, then work out the square root of 12.5, which ... requires a calculator! That's why it's easiest to use a 3-4-5 triangle, like this, which conveniently works with whole numbers. And that's also why I'm measuring in **imperial**, because 3 feet by 4 feet by 5 feet is a practical size to work with.

8.1 Write the numbers in words. Look at A opposite to help you.

1 1.793 ..... one ..... point ..... seven ..... nine ..... three .....
2 1/100 mm ..... One ..... hundreth ..... of ..... a ..... millimetre
3 1/1000 mm ..... one ..... thousemdth ..... of ..... a ..... millimetre
4 0 ..... Zero ..... or ..... naught .....

8.2 Complete the descriptions of the numbers using words from A opposite.

1 0.25 = ¼   The first number is a decimal, and the second is a ..... fraction ..... .

2 0.6368 ≈ 0.637   The second number is ..... rounded ..... up ..... to three ..... decimal places ..... .

3 7.5278 ≈ 7.5   The second number is ..... rounded ..... down ..... to one ..... decimal place ..... .

4 8, 26, 154   The numbers aren't fractions or decimals. They're ..... whole ..... numbers.

5 Error: 0.00001%   The error is so small that it's ..... negligible .....

6 0.586 kg × 9,000 = 5,274 kg
     0.59 kg × 9,000 = 5,310 kg   This difference is the result of a ..... rounding ..... error ..... .

8.3 Complete the calculations using the words in the box. Sometimes there is more than one possible answer. Look at B opposite to help you.

divided	minus	plus	square root	subtract	times
less	multiplied	square	squared	sum	

1 14 + 8 = 22   Fourteen ..... plus ..... eight equals twenty-two.
2 100 × 20 = 2,000   One hundred ..... times ..... twenty is two thousand.
3 7 × 11 = 77   Seven ..... multiplied ..... by eleven equals seventy-seven.
4 400 ÷ 8 = 50   Four hundred ..... divided ..... by eight equals fifty.
5 95 + 2 = 97   The ..... sum ..... of ninety-five and two is ninety-seven.
6 8² = 64   The ..... square ..... of eight is sixty-four.
7 50 − 30 = 20   If you ..... substract ..... thirty from fifty, it equals twenty.
8 √100 = 10   The ..... square root ..... of a hundred is ten.
9 11² = 121   Eleven ..... squared ..... is a hundred and twenty-one.
10 48 − 12 = 36   Forty-eight ..... minus ..... twelve equals thirty-six.

8.4 Use your knowledge of basic geometry to complete the sentences. Use one or two words from B opposite to fill each gap.

1 The ..... sum ..... of the three angles in a triangle equals 180 degrees.
2 The area of a circle is equal to the ..... square ..... of its radius ..... times ..... 3.14.
3 The area of a right-angle triangle is equal to the length of one adjacent side, ... times ..... the length of the other adjacent side, ... divided ..... two.
4 The length of each side of a square is equal to the ..... square root ..... of the square's area.
5 If each angle in a triangle is 60°, then the lengths of its sides are ..... equal ..... .

Over to you

Write down a few examples of some calculations you did recently, or ones that you do frequently, and then explain them.

9 Area, size and mass

A Area

The textbook extract below looks at different aspects of **area**.

Dimensions of wires and cables

The sizes of electrical wires are specified by a number which gives an area in **square millimetres**. For example, in a home, a 6 mm² wire may be specified to supply an electric oven in a kitchen. This number gives the **cross-sectional area** of the conductor. Increasing the cross-sectional area allows the conductor to carry more current safely, without overheating.

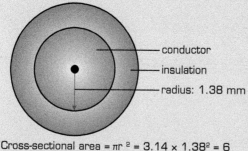

conductor
insulation
radius: 1.38 mm

Cross-sectional area = $\pi r^2 = 3.14 \times 1.38^2 = 6$

▲ *Cross-section of 6 mm² wire*

In high-voltage power lines, it is not only the cross-sectional area of conductors that is important, but also their **surface area** – the amount of surface that is in contact with the air, to allow cooling. Therefore, instead of using single cables with large sections for each conductor, power lines often use groups of two, three or four **small-section** cables, to give more surface area than a single, **large-section** cable.

B Weight, mass, volume and density

In everyday language, the term **weight** means how heavy things are (how much they **weigh**), and **grams** and **kilograms** are used as units of weight. But in physics and in engineering, grams and kilograms are units of **mass**. Whether an object is on earth – where it is subjected to **gravity** (the pull of the earth) – or floating **weightless** in space, its mass is always the same. The mass of an object depends on:

- the **volume** of the object, measured in **cubic metres** (m³) – as an object's volume increases, its mass increases

- the **density** of the object, measured in **kilograms per cubic metre** (kg/m³) – as density increases, mass **per unit of volume** increases.

The mass of an object is the object's volume multiplied by its density. The weight of an object is the force exerted on the object's mass by gravity.

Some materials are very **dense**, and therefore very heavy. An example is lead (Pb), which has a density of 11,340 kg/m³. Other materials, such as expanded polystyrene (which can have a density as low as 10 kg/m³), are very **lightweight**.

9.1 The component below is made of mild steel. It has a radius of 40 mm and it is 1,200 mm long. Complete the calculations using the words in the box. Look at A and B opposite to help you.

cross-sectional area	density	mass	surface area	volume

(1) .... of mild steel: 7,850 kg/m³

(2)............................ : πr² = 3.14 × 40² = 5 024 mm² = 0.005024 m²

(3) .... : 0.005024 m² × 1.2 m = 0.0060288 m³

(4) .... : 0.0060288 m³ × 7,850 kg/m³ = 47.32608 kg

Circumference: 2πr = 3.14 × 40 mm = 251 mm = 0.251 m

Total (5) .... to be painted: 0.251 m × 1.2 m + 0.005 m² + 0.005 m² = 0.311 m²

9.2 Now write the whole words for the unit abbreviations in the calculation in 9.1 above. Look at A and B opposite to help you. The first one has been done for you.

1 m   metres   4 m²   7 kg/m³
2 mm   5 m³
3 mm²   6 kg

9.3 Complete the extract from an article about satellite design using the words in the box. Look at A and B opposite to help you.

cubic	gravity	lightweight	mass	square	weigh	weightless

Satellites need to be designed to cope with two very different phases: deployment (the journey into space by rocket) and operation (working in space).

For the first phase, engineers are faced with the problem that every (1) .... metre of volume taken up within the rocket will add millions of dollars to its ticket into space. And each extra gram of (2) .... added to the craft will increase the fuel needed to propel it upwards against the pull of (3) .... That extra fuel, in turn, will (4) .... a little more, further adding to the total weight of the craft. With the cost of kilograms so high, the satellite must therefore be as (5) .... as possible.

In the second phase, with the orbiting satellite now (6) ...., its mass is practically irrelevant. As for the amount of space occupied, the situation is completely reversed. The satellite's solar panels, which transform sunlight into battery power, must unfold to cover as wide an area as possible – opening out to cover an area of several (7) .... metres – in order to maximize their exposure to the sun.

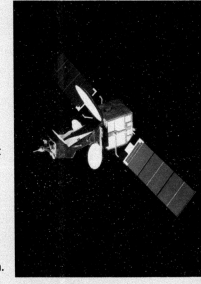

Over to you

Talk about different materials that are suitable for specific engineering uses due to their density – because they are either very dense, or very lightweight.

10 Measurable parameters

A Supply, demand and capacity

The article below is from the technology section of a business magazine.

Technology

Calculating the **capacity** of an electricity grid – the amount of energy it needs to **supply** to users – might seem simple. Just add up the power supplied over a given **period** of time to give the total amount **consumed** by users. Then, divide the **cumulative** amount of power used during the whole period by the number of hours in the period. The result is an **average** level of **consumption** per hour. But there's one problem with this method – and it's a major one.

The **rate** of power consumption – the amount that's being consumed at a particular moment – is not **constant**. In other words, consumption does not stay at the same level all the time. So electricity **supply** requirements cannot simply be **averaged out** over time. People use more power at certain times of day, and less at other times, which means that **demand** for power **fluctuates** significantly. Generally, it rises to a maximum in the evening (**peak** demand is at evening mealtimes), and falls to its lowest levels during the night. These **fluctuations** are so big that at **peak times** consumption can be twice as high as it is during **off-peak times**. Clearly, the grid needs to have sufficient capacity to **meet demand** when consumption **peaks**. But since each peak is brief, the grid will only **run to capacity** – at or close to its maximum capability – for a few moments each day. This means, most of the time, it has significant **spare capacity**.

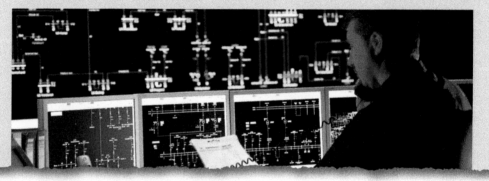

B Input, output and efficiency

Power lines and transformers are relatively **inefficient**, wasting energy – mainly by giving off heat. As a result, there is a difference between **input** – the amount of energy put into the grid by power stations, and **output** – the amount used by consumers. On a typical grid, the difference between input and output is about 7% – there is a 7% energy **loss**. But if electricity is generated at the place where it's consumed, and not transmitted through long-distance power lines, this loss can be avoided. Consequently, locally produced electricity is more **efficient** than grid-supplied power, as there is a **gain** in **efficiency** of around 7%.

Photovoltaic solar panels

One way to produce power locally is with photovoltaics (PVs) – often called solar panels. However, many PV installations are still connected to the electricity grid. This means that when there is **surplus** power – when electricity is being produced by the solar panels faster than it is needed in the home – it is fed <u>into</u> the grid. If consumption **exceeds** production – if electricity is being used in the home faster than the solar panels can produce it – then power is taken <u>from</u> the grid. Homes with low consumption may therefore become **net** producers of power, producing more electricity than they consume.

10.1 An engineer is talking to a colleague about the design of a fuel tank for a water pump. Complete the explanation using the words in the box. Look at A opposite to help you.

average	constant	consumption	duration
capacity	consume	cumulative	rate

Fuel (1) .... for this engine is about 1.5 litres per hour. Of course, sometimes it'll (2) .... a bit more, sometimes a bit less, depending on the workload. But 1.5 is an (3) .... figure. And let's say the (4) .... of a work shift is 8 hours. The pump will have to be stopped occasionally, to clean the intake filter, so it won't be 8 hours of (5) .... running. But we'll say 8 hours, to be on the safe side. So 8 hours of running at a (6) .... of 1.5 litres per hour gives 12 litres of (7) .... consumption over a shift. So if we want the pump to have sufficient fuel autonomy for an 8-hour shift, the (8) .... of the fuel tank needs to be 12 litres, minimum.

10.2 The graph below shows water consumption in a washing process at a manufacturing plant. Write figures to complete the comments. Look at A opposite to help you.

1 Water consumption fluctuated between .... and .... litres per second.
2 Averaged out over the period shown, consumption was roughly .... litres per second.
3 Consumption peaked at a rate of .... litres per second.
4 If the process ran to capacity, it could use water at a rate of .... litres per second.
5 When consumption peaked, the process had spare capacity of .... litres per second.

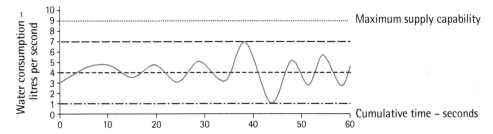

10.3 Choose the correct words from the brackets to complete the explanations from a guided tour of a manufacturing plant. Look at A and B opposite to help you.

1 A lot of heat is generated in this part of the process. And all of that (input / output) is recycled – it provides a (demand / supply) of heat for the next stage of the process. So it's quite an (efficient / inefficient) system.
2 Sometimes, there's (insufficient / surplus) heat, and it can't all be recycled. At other times there isn't quite enough recycled heat to keep up with (peak / off-peak) demand for heat energy further along the process.
3 Some material is lost in the washing process, but the mass of water absorbed is greater than the mass of material lost. So there's a net (loss / gain) in total mass.

Over to you

Think of an energy-consuming appliance you're familiar with. Imagine you are starting a project to redesign it, in order to improve its efficiency. Answer the following questions:

● How much energy does the appliance consume? Is consumption constant or fluctuating? Describe any fluctuations, in terms of average and peak consumption.

● How efficient is the appliance? What are the main reasons for inefficiencies? What are your first thoughts on how efficiency could be improved?

11 Material types

Metals and non-metals

Engineering materials can be divided into:

- **metals** – examples of **metallic** materials are iron (Fe) and copper (Cu)
- **non-metals** – examples of **non-metallic** materials are carbon (C) and silicon (Si).

As iron is such a widely used material, metals can be divided into:

- **ferrous metals** – those that contain iron
- **non-ferrous metals** – those that do not contain iron.

B Elements, compounds and mixtures

With regard to the **chemical composition** of materials – the chemicals they contain, and how those chemicals are combined – three main categories can be used:

- **Elements** are pure materials in their most basic form. They cannot be broken down into different **constituents** ('ingredients'). Examples of elements widely used in engineering materials are iron, carbon and aluminium (Al).

- **Compounds** consist of two or more elements that are **chemically bound** – that is, combined by a chemical reaction. An everyday example is water, which is **a compound of** hydrogen (H) and oxygen (O).

- **Mixtures** consist of two or more elements or compounds which are mixed together, but which are not chemically bound. In engineering, common examples are **alloys** – that is, metals which have other metals and/or non-metals mixed with them. A common example is steel, which is an **iron–carbon alloy**, and can include other **alloying metals** – metals which are added to alloys, in small quantities relative to the main metal. Examples of widely used alloying metals are chromium (Cr), manganese (Mn) and tungsten (W).

> BrE: aluminium /ˌæl.jʊˈmɪn.i.əm/; AmE: aluminum /əˈluː.mɪ.nəm/

Note: For a list of chemical elements and their symbols, see Appendix IV on page 104.

C Composite materials

The article below is from an engineering journal.

Materials under the microscope: composites

When you think of examples of hi-tech materials, **composite materials** come to mind – such as carbon-fibre, used in aerospace and Formula 1 cars. But although we think of **composites** as hi-tech and highly expensive, that's not always true. The earliest examples of composite materials were bricks made from mud and straw. Or, to use the correct composite terms, from straw **reinforcement** – the structural network that reinforces the material inside, and a mud **matrix** – the material surrounding the reinforcement. These terms explain what a composite material is: a matrix with a **reinforcing material** inside it. A modern, everyday example is fibreglass – correctly called **glass-reinforced plastic (GRP)** – which has a plastic matrix **reinforced with** glass fibres.

11.1 Complete the sentences using the words in the box. Look at A opposite and Appendix IV on page 104 to help you.

| metal | non-metal | metallic | non-metallic | ferrous | non-ferrous |

1 Carbon (C) is a ....
2 Copper (Cu) is a .... metal.
3 Aluminium (Al) is a common ....
4 Steel (Fe + C) is a widely used .... metal.
5 Although it is used in steel, carbon is ....
6 Aluminium is relatively lightweight for a .... material.

11.2 Decide whether the sentences below are true or false, and correct the false sentences. Look at B opposite to help you.

1 The elements that make up a compound are chemically bound.
2 Alloys are chemical compounds that are frequently used in engineering.
3 Alloys can contain both metallic and non-metallic constituents.
4 In an alloy, an alloying metal is the biggest constituent, by percentage.
5 Steel is a metallic element.

11.3 Complete the extract about concrete and steel, using suitable forms of the word *reinforce* from C opposite. Sometimes there is more than one possible answer.

(1) .... concrete is one of the most widely used construction materials, and one we take for granted. However, using steel bars to (2) .... concrete structures located outdoors is only possible thanks to a fortunate coincidence: concrete and steel have practically the same coefficient of thermal expansion – in other words, as atmospheric temperature varies, the concrete and the steel (3) .... expand and contract at the same rate, allowing uniform movement. Using a (4) .... material with a different coefficient of expansion would not be feasible. For example, (5) aluminium-...............................concrete would quickly disintegrate.

11.4 Read the text below and find two elements, two compounds, an alloy and a composite. Look at A, B and C opposite to help you.

Generally, the steel used in reinforced concrete will have previously been exposed to water and to the oxygen in the air. As a result, it will usually be partly corroded, being covered with a layer of iron oxide (rust). However, once the steel is inside the hardened concrete, it will be protected from air and water, which prevents further rusting. Additionally, the cement in concrete does not react aggressively with the iron in steel.

Element	Compound	Alloy	Composite

Over to you

Think of some of the materials used to make products or structures you know about. Say whether the materials are elements, compounds, mixtures, alloys or composites. If they are composites, what materials are used (a) as the matrix, and (b) as reinforcement?

12 Steel

A Carbon steels

This extract from an article in an engineering journal is about different types of steel.

Steel is the most widely used engineering material. Technically, though, this well-known alloy of **iron** and **carbon** is not as simple as one might think. Steel comes in a huge range of different **grades**, each with different characteristics. For the inexperienced, it can be difficult to know where to begin.

A good place to start is with the two main types of steel. The first, **carbon steels**, consist of iron and carbon, and contain no significant quantities of other metals. Carbon steels can be divided into three main grades:

- **Mild steel** – the most widely used grade – is a low carbon steel which contains up to approximately 0.3% carbon.
- **Medium carbon steel** contains between approximately 0.3% and 0.6% carbon.
- **High carbon steel** contains between approximately 0.6% and 1.4% carbon.

Note: The chemical symbol for iron = Fe, and carbon = C.

B Alloy steels

The article goes on to look at **alloy steels**.

The second main category of steel is alloy steels, which consist of iron, carbon and one or more alloying metals. Specific grades of alloy steel include:

- **low alloy steels**, which contain 90% or more iron, and up to approximately 10% of alloying metals such as **chromium, nickel, manganese, molybdenum** and **vanadium**
- **high strength low alloy steels (HSLA)**, which contain smaller quantities of the above metals (typically less than 2%)
- **stainless steels**, which contain chromium as well as other metals – such as nickel – and which do not **rust**.
- **tool steels**, which are extremely hard, and are used in cutting tools. They contain **tungsten** and/or **cobalt**. A widely used grade of tool steel is **high-speed steel**, which is used in cutting tools that operate at high temperatures, such as drill bits.

Notes: The terms **carbon steel** and **alloy steel** can cause confusion, as carbon steels are also alloys, and alloy steels also contain carbon.
The chemical symbol for chromium = Cr, cobalt = Co, nickel = Ni, manganese = Mn, molybdenum = Mo, tungsten = W, and vanadium = V.

C Corrosion

One weakness of mild steel is that it **corrodes** – its surface progressively deteriorates due to a chemical reaction. This reaction takes place between the iron in the steel and the oxygen (O_2) in the air, to form **iron oxide**. When iron corrodes, we say that it rusts. In some metals, such as aluminium (Al), the presence of **corrosion** is not a problem, as the layer of **oxide** around the metal remains hard, which prevents it from **oxidizing** any further. However, when mild steel **goes rusty**, the **rust** on the surface comes off continuously, and a new **rusty** layer forms, progressively 'eating into' the metal.

12.1 Decide whether the sentences below are true or false, and correct the false sentences. Look at A and B opposite to help you.

1 Steel is an alloy of iron and carbon.
2 Mild steel is a high carbon steel.
3 Alloy steels contain carbon.
4 Chromium and nickel are used as alloying metals in steel.
5 Low alloy steels contain more chromium than iron.
6 Stainless steel is an alloy steel.
7 Tungsten is added to steel to make it softer.
8 High-speed steel is suitable for making cutting tools that get very hot.

12.2 Complete the table with words related to *corrode, oxide* and *rust*. Then use the words to complete the sentences below. There is more than one possible answer. Look at C opposite to help you.

Verb	Noun	Adjective
		corroded
		oxidized
/ go rusty		

1 When steel is exposed to air and water, it ....
2 A brown/red material on the surface of steel is called ....
3 The strength of steel is reduced if it is ....

12.3 Complete the article about a special type of steel, using words from A, B and C opposite.

Weathering steel

The perennial problem with mild (1) .... is that it (2) .... when exposed to air and water. Generally, the only solution is either to apply a protective coating, or to use another (3) .... of steel that is resistant to the (4) .... process – the most well-known being (5) .... steel, which contains significant quantities of (6) .... and, often, nickel.

There is, however, an alternative solution. So-called weathering steel is a special alloy suitable for outdoor use. But rather than being completely protected from corrosion, the surface of the steel is allowed to go (7) .... Once a layer of (8) .... has formed on the surface, it stabilizes and forms a hard protective layer. This layer differs from ordinary (9) .... oxide, as it does not continue to eat into the metal. While not everyone may like the 'rusty look', weathering steel has been widely used in architectural applications and outdoor sculptures.

 Over to you

Think about some items you're familiar with that are made of steel, but which are not protected (for example, by paint). How serious is the potential problem of corrosion? How is it prevented or limited – for example, by using a specific grade of steel?

13 Non-ferrous metals

A Common non-ferrous engineering metals

These website extracts look at the engineering applications of some **non-ferrous metals** – that is, metals that do not contain iron.

Aluminium is widely used, often in alloy forms. An example is duralumin, an alloy used in aircraft manufacturing, which also contains **copper** (4.4%) and **magnesium** (1.5%). Aluminium can also be alloyed with **titanium** to produce very strong, lightweight metals.

Copper is an excellent electrical conductor, which makes it ideal for use in electric wires. Good ductility also makes it suitable for pipes. Copper is widely used in alloys, notably **brass** (copper and **zinc**) and **bronze** (copper and **tin**, and sometimes **lead**).

Silver is a **precious metal** – a reference to its high cost. It is a better electrical conductor than any other material, so it is often used for electronic connections. Another precious metal – **gold** – is also an excellent conductor, and is highly corrosion-resistant.

Notes: For more on metals and alloys, see Unit 11. For more on **ductility**, see Unit 18.
The chemical symbol for aluminium = Al, copper = Cu, magnesium = Mg, titanium = Ti, zinc = Zn, tin = Sn, lead = Pb, silver = Ag and gold = Au.

B Plating with non-ferrous metals

Non-ferrous metals can be used to protect steel from corrosion by **plating** it – that is, covering it with a thin layer of metal. An example is **galvanizing** (zinc plating).

Steel can be **hot-dip galvanized,** by placing it in **molten** (liquid) zinc. It can also be **electro-galvanized**, which is a type of **electroplating.** With this technique, the steel component is placed in a liquid (often an acid) – called the **electrolyte** – and connected to the **negative terminal** (–) of an electrical supply, to become the **cathode** (the negative side). A piece of zinc is also placed in the electrolyte, and is connected to the **positive terminal** (+) of the supply. This then becomes the **anode** (the positive side). An electric current then flows between the pieces of metal, through the electrolyte. This causes a chemical reaction, which deposits zinc on the cathode, plating the component.

A related process, called **anodizing**, is used to protect aluminium. The component to be **anodized** is connected to the positive terminal (to become the anode) and placed in an electrolyte, with a cathode. As electricity flows, **aluminium oxide** is deposited on the anode. As this is harder than aluminium metal, it provides protection.

13.1 Make correct sentences using one part from each column. Look at A opposite to help you. The first one has been done for you.

1 Duralumin	can be mixed with copper to make	silver.
2 Titanium	resists corrosion better than the other precious metal,	brass.
3 Zinc	has a high strength-to-weight ratio and is often alloyed with	aluminium.
4 Copper	is an aluminium alloy that also contains copper and	bronze.
5 Gold	can be mixed with tin and lead to produce	magnesium.

13.2 Complete the word groups below using the names of the metals in 13.1 above. You will need to write some names more than once. Look at A opposite to help you.

Metal elements	
Alloys	
Precious metals	

13.3 Complete the checklist for electroplating using the words in the box. Look at B opposite to help you.

| anode | electrolyte | galvanizing | plated |
| cathode | electroplating | negative | positive |

✓ Check that there is sufficient (1) .... in the bath to completely cover the component, in order to ensure that the component will subsequently be (2) .... over its entire surface area.

✓ Ensure that the component is connected to the (3) .... terminal of the electrical supply. During the (4) .... process, the component should function as the (5) ....

✓ Ensure that the metal being used for plating – e.g. zinc for (6) .... – is connected to the (7) .... terminal of the electrical supply. During the process, it should function as the (8) ....

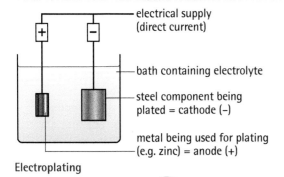

Electroplating

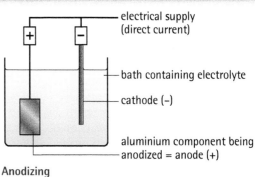

Anodizing

Over to you

How are non-ferrous metals used in your industry, or an industry you're familiar with? Is electroplating common? If so, what kinds of metals are used for plating, and why are these specific metals chosen?

14 Polymers

A Natural and synthetic polymers

The web page below, from a website for engineering students, provides an introduction to polymers.

With names such as polytetrafluoroethyline and polyethyleneteraphthalate, it's not surprising that polymers are usually called by their more common name, **plastic**. But what, exactly, is a polymer or a plastic?

Polymers are compounds made up of several elements that are chemically bound. Most compounds consist of large numbers of tiny **molecules**, which each contain just a few **atoms**. For example, a water molecule – H_2O – contains two hydrogen atoms and one oxygen atom. But the molecules of polymers contain huge numbers of atoms, joined together in long **chains**.

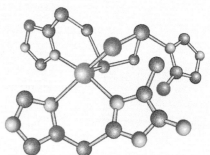

A polymer chain

Rubber, thanks to its many uses from rubber bands to car tyres, is one of the best-known polymers. It comes from **latex**, a **natural** liquid which comes from rubber trees. Rubber is therefore a **natural polymer**. However, most of the polymers used in industry are not natural, but **synthetic**. The term 'plastic' is generally used to refer to **synthetic polymers** – in other words, those that are **manmade**.

Note: **Rubber** can be natural (**natural rubber**) or synthetic (**synthetic rubber**).

B Thermoplastics and thermosetting plastics

The page goes on to look at types of polymer.

Synthetic polymers can be divided into two main categories:

Thermoplastics can be melted by heat, and formed in shaped containers called **moulds**. After the liquid plastic has cooled, it **sets** to form a solid material. A thermoplastic is a type of plastic that can be heated and **moulded** numerous times. Examples of thermoplastics that are common in engineering include:
- **ABS** (acrylonitrile butadiene styrene) – stiff and light, used in vehicle bodywork
- **polycarbonate** – used to make strong, transparent panels and vehicle lights
- **PVC** (polyvinylchloride) – a cheaper plastic used for window frames and pipes.

Thermosetting plastics, also called **thermosets**, can be heated and moulded like thermoplastics. They may also be mixed from cold ingredients. However, during cooling or mixing, a chemical reaction occurs, causing thermosets to **cure**. This means they set permanently, and cannot be moulded again. If a thermoset is heated after curing, it will burn. Examples of thermosets used in engineering are:
- **epoxy resins** – used in very strong adhesives
- **polyimides** – strong and flexible, used as insulators in some electric cables.

Two more categories of polymer are **engineering plastics** and **elastomers**. Engineering plastics are mostly thermoplastics that are especially strong, such as ABS and polycarbonate. Elastomers are very elastic polymers which can be stretched by force to at least twice their original length, and can then return to their original length when the force is removed.

14.1 Circle the correct words to complete the text. Look at A opposite to help you.

> A lot of rubber is made from latex, a (1) *natural/synthetic* polymer which comes from rubber trees. However, not all rubber comes from trees. Synthetic rubber is a (2) *manmade/natural* polymer with similar properties to latex. Plastics are also polymers. Like rubber, they consist of long chains of (3) *atoms/molecules* which form extremely large (4) *atoms/molecules*.

14.2 Read the extract describing a plastic panel manufacturing process. Then decide whether the sentences below are true or false, and correct the false sentences. Look at B opposite to help you.

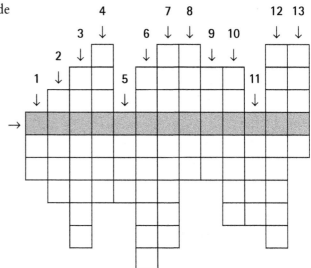

> By this stage of the process, the plastic is solid, and has fully cooled. Selected panels can now undergo quality-control testing, to check they are strong enough to cope with the tough conditions they will be exposed to in use. Tests include tensile testing, where narrow lengths of panel are subjected to high tension loads to check they do not stretch or fracture. More tests are carried out to check the panels' resistance to impacts and scratching. Any products that fail the tests are returned to the beginning of the production process, melted down, and their material is reused.

1 The plastic was heated earlier in the process.
2 The plastic has now set.
3 The plastic is now liquid.
4 To pass one of the tests, the plastic must be an elastomer.
5 The description suggests the plastic is a type of engineering plastic.
6 The material is a thermosetting plastic.
7 The material is a thermoplastic.

14.3 Complete the word puzzle and find the word going across the page. Look at A and B opposite to help you.

1 a shorter name for polyvinylchloride
2 used for forming melted plastic
3 a group of atoms
4 a long chain of atoms
5 to set permanently
6 a very elastic polymer
7 a plastic that sets permanently
8 a natural polymer
9 a very strong thermoset resin
10 not natural
11 particles that form molecules
12 another word for 'not natural'
13 material used to make rubber

15 Minerals and ceramics

A Mineral and ceramic engineering materials

A **mineral** is a natural, **inorganic** material (one that is not living) which is found in the ground, often within rocks. Minerals are quite pure. Rocks, on the other hand, can be mixtures of several minerals, and may also contain previously **organic** material. Examples of minerals include different types of **ore** – from which metal can be extracted – such as **iron ore**. Non-metallic minerals include:

- **diamond**, an extremely hard form of **carbon** (C), which is used as an **abrasive** (very hard and rough) material in cutting tools – frequently referred to as **industrial diamond** when used in engineering
- **silicon** (Si), found in sand as **silica** (silicon dioxide – SiO_2), which can be heated to high temperatures to make glass.

Generally, inorganic, non-metallic materials that have been formed by heating are called **ceramics**. Glass is therefore a ceramic. When materials are heated to extremely high temperatures to form ceramics that are **glass-like** – that is, with a structure like that of glass – we say that they are **vitrified**.

Clay bricks

Ceramic materials are used to make construction materials such as **bricks**. These are made from **clay**, and are then **fired** in a **kiln** – that is, heated to a high temperature in an industrial oven. Clay can also be vitrified – for example, to make waterproof pipes.

B Glass

A technical adviser for a glass manufacturer is giving a briefing to a group of engineers at a trade fair.

'**Sheets** of glass, which are obviously flat and thin, are called **float glass**. This refers to the manufacturing technique where molten glass is floated on molten tin, to produce flat sheets. Usually, after float glass has been formed, it's **annealed** – it's left to cool slowly. But if it's left in this state, and the glass later gets broken, it breaks into dangerous, sharp pieces. So for most engineering and architectural uses, **annealed glass** is unsuitable. We need to use what we call **safety glass**.'

'One type of safety glass is **toughened glass**, also called **tempered glass**. As the term suggests, the glass is tempered – it's heated and kept hot for a certain time, to change its structure. Then if tempered glass is broken, it **shatters** – it breaks into tiny pieces. These are a lot safer than the long, sharp pieces produced when annealed glass breaks. The disadvantage of toughened glass is that it can't withstand impacts from small objects, such as flying stones. So, for instance, that makes it unsuitable for vehicle **windscreens**. So in cases where impacts are a problem, another type of safety glass – **laminated glass** – is generally used. This is made by **laminating** glass **with** a polymer – in other words, making a glass and polymer 'sandwich', with a sheet of polymer in the middle and sheets of glass at either side. The advantage of having a **laminated** material is not just that it's very strong. The **layers** of glass are **bonded to** a layer of polymer – they're stuck to the polymer – so if the glass does break, the broken pieces are held together, and don't fly.'

> BrE: windscreen; AmE: windshield

15.1 Decide whether the sentences below are true or false. Then, change one word in each of the false sentences to correct them. Look at A opposite to help you.

1 Minerals are organic.
2 Minerals can be found in rocks.
3 Silica is a compound containing silicon.
4 Minerals can be metallic or non-metallic.
5 Industrial diamond is an abrasive, metallic mineral.
6 In order to become ceramics, materials must be vitrified.
7 Clay can be fired to produce material with a glass-like structure.

15.2 Use the words and expressions in the box to describe each photo. You will need to use some words more than once. Look at B opposite to help you.

annealed glass	safety glass	toughened glass
laminated glass	tempered glass	windscreen

1

2

3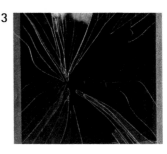

....

15.3 Complete the article about bulletproof glass from a science and technology magazine, using words from B opposite. Sometimes, more than one word is possible.

'Bulletproof' is a loosely used word, suggesting something is totally unbreakable. But technically speaking, how accurate is the term 'bulletproof glass'? Outside of Hollywood movies, can glass really stop bullets? The answer is, not on its own. But if several (1) .... of glass are sandwiched with a high-strength polymer to form (2) .... glass, a bullet-resistant, if not completely bulletproof, barrier can be obtained.

The technique of sandwiching polymer and glass is nothing unusual. Car windscreens are made by (3) .... glass to a polymer, such as polyvinyl butyral (PVB), to form a type of safety glass. Unlike the other main type of safety glass – (4) .... glass – laminated glass remains intact on breaking. If a stone hits a windscreen, even though a small section of the glass on the outside may crack, the polymer behind it will stop the stone, and also ensure the entire piece of glass doesn't (5) .... Bullet-resistant glass uses the same principle, but must be much tougher. A stronger polymer is therefore used – often polycarbonate – as well as a greater number of (6) .... of glass and polymer.

Over to you

Think about the different ceramics and minerals used in your industry, or in an industry you're familiar with. What types of material are used, and why?

16 Concrete

A Concrete mix design

Cement

Sand – fine aggregate

Gravel – coarse aggregate

Cement is a key material in construction. It consists of a very fine powder. When water is added to cement, a chemical reaction occurs, and the cement begins to **set** – it starts to become solid. The most widely used **cement-based** material is **concrete**, which is made from cement, **fine aggregate** (sand), **coarse aggregate** (gravel) and water. After concrete has set, it needs time to reach its **structural strength** – the strength needed to perform effectively. Generally, engineers consider that this strength is reached after 28 days – a point called **28-day strength**.

Concrete **mix designs**, which are specified by engineers, state the proportions of cement, fine aggregate and coarse aggregate to be used for specific structures. For example, a **1:2:4 (one-two-four)** mix consists of one **part** cement, two parts fine aggregate and four parts coarse aggregate. For mixing precise quantities – known as **batching** – proportions are measured by weight. Mix designs also specify the **water–cement ratio** – the amount of water added relative to the amount of cement used. Excess water reduces the strength of concrete, so the quantity of water is kept to a minimum. But as drier concrete is more difficult to work with, an **additive** (added chemical substance) called a **plasticizer** is often used. This helps the concrete to flow more easily. Other additives can also be used – for example, a **retarder** may be added to delay setting, which gives workers more time to **pour** (place) the concrete.

B Reinforced concrete

Reinforced concrete (**RC**) structures contain steel bars. Steel **reinforcement** is needed mainly because concrete is weak in tension – that is, bad at resisting stretching forces. As steel is strong in tension, **reinforcing bars** overcome this weakness.

In order to form the different parts of structures, **formwork** – sometimes also called **shuttering** – is used. This consists of moulds of the required size and shape, made from steel or timber, which are used to contain the concrete until it has set.

In-situ reinforced concrete being poured

When wet concrete is **cast** (placed) in its final position, it is called **in-situ concrete**. Instead of being **cast in-situ**, reinforced concrete elements can also be **precast** – cast at a factory – then delivered to the construction site ready for assembly. Sometimes, **precast concrete** is also **prestressed**. With **prestressing**, tension is applied to the reinforcing bars, by machine, usually before the concrete is poured. The bars are then held in tension while wet concrete is poured around them. After the concrete has fully set, the bars become 'trapped' in tension. This increases the concrete's ability to resist bending forces.

16.1 Find words and expressions in A opposite to match the descriptions (1–10).

1 gravel used in concrete ....
2 sand used in concrete ....
3 powder that enables concrete to set ....
4 mixing concrete accurately ....
5 specification of concrete ingredients ....
6 effective structural capability of concrete ....-............................ ....
7 affects the wetness and strength of concrete ....—............................ ....
8 different types of chemical put in concrete ....
9 allows concrete to stay wet for longer ....
10 makes drier concrete easier to work with ....

16.2 Complete the textbook extract about a type of prestressed concrete using the words in the box. Look at B opposite to help you.

cast	formwork	pouring	prestressing	structural
concrete	in-situ	precast	reinforcement	

Prestressing techniques

In the production of reinforced concrete components, the process of (1) .... usually involves holding the (2) .... in tension while (3) .... the concrete. This form of prestressing is called pre-tensioning, as tension is applied *before* the concrete is poured. The technique is often used in the manufacture of floor components, which are small enough to fit on the back of a truck, and can therefore be (4) .... at a factory.

A less common prestressing technique is post-tensioning (applying tension *after* the concrete has set). This is more suitable for large elements, especially long beams, which cannot be transported, and therefore need to be poured (5) .... Before the concrete is poured, ducts (usually plastic tubes) are placed inside the (6) .... along the length of the beam. These ducts contain steel cables. After the concrete has been (7) .... and has gained sufficient (8) .... strength, the cables are put in tension, using jacks at either end of the beam. This is only possible because the cables are free to move within the ducts – it is not possible with pre-tensioned reinforcing bars, which are held fast by the hard (9) .... surrounding them. The ends of the cables are then permanently anchored at either end of the beam.

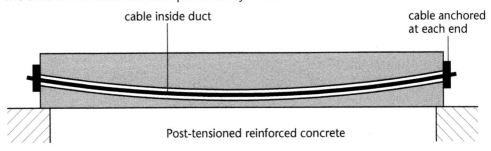

cable inside duct

cable anchored at each end

Post-tensioned reinforced concrete

Over to you

Think about a reinforced concrete structure in your area – for example, a building or a bridge. In what sequence do you think it was built? Do you think it was poured in-situ, or were its parts precast?

17 Wood

A Categories of wood

The two main categories of **wood** are:

- **hardwood** – usually from deciduous trees, which lose their leaves in autumn, although some hardwood (for example, tropical hardwood) comes from other types of tree

- **softwood** – from coniferous trees, which remain green throughout the year.

In engineering, wood can be categorized as:

- **solid wood** – softwood or hardwood that has been sawn into specific shapes and sizes, but whose natural structure, consisting of **grain** and **knots**, remains intact

- **engineered wood** – made by **bonding** (sticking together) layers of solid softwood or hardwood, or by mixing quantities of wood particles and bonding them with resin.

Notes: In industry, wood is often referred to as **timber** (BrE) or **lumber** (AmE).
In American English, **timber** generally means wood that is still growing in trees.
Knot is pronounced /nɒt/ (the k is silent).

B Solid structural timber

The text below is from a technical handbook about **structural timber** – wood intended to support loads in a structure.

Generally, timber is cut to the required **section** – the width and depth that determine its cross-section – at a **sawmill**, where a range of section sizes are produced. Timber from sawmills is generally supplied in **rough-sawn** sections. This refers to the surface texture produced by **sawing** timber with a **circular saw**. If the timber needs to have a smooth finish – for example, because it will be visible in the structure – it can subsequently be **planed** to smooth its surface.

Because the strength of wood varies, structural timber must be **stress-graded**. This means its strength is tested in order to give it a **stress grade** – a standard strength value which an engineer can use for design calculations. Timber can be **mechanically stress-graded**, where its strength is checked by machine. It can also be **visually stress-graded**, where the wood is examined by an inspector who looks for potential weaknesses – in particular, the position of knots.

C Engineered wood

Engineered wood covers a range of softwood and hardwood materials. It includes:

- cheap, low-strength **boards**, such as **particle board** (often called **chipboard**) and **medium-density fibreboard (MDF)**

- stronger boards suitable for structural use – primarily **orientated strand board (OSB)**, which is made from strands of wood bonded with resin, and **plywood**, which consists of several **plies** (layers) of solid wood, bonded so that the grain of each ply **runs** at 90 degrees to that of the adjacent plies, to provide increased strength

- **glue-laminated** sections – sometimes called **glulams** – which can be used as major structural elements, such as beams, in large buildings.

Particle board or chipboard

Orientated strand board (OSB)

Plywood

17.1 Match the two parts to make correct sentences about wood. In each case, there is more than one possible answer. Look at A opposite to help you.

1 Engineered wood
2 Softwood
3 Solid wood

a comes only from coniferous trees.
b comes only from deciduous trees.
c can come from either coniferous or deciduous trees.
d specifically describes single pieces of timber, not multiple pieces that have been bonded together.
e is always made from multiple pieces or particles of wood.
f may have knots in it.

17.2 Complete the sentences below using words and expressions from B opposite.

1 Wood has a smooth finish after it has been ....
2 Wood cut with a circular saw is called .... timber.
3 After timber is tested for strengths and weaknesses, it is given a ....
4 When timber is inspected by a person who looks for weaknesses, it is

....
5 When timber is inspected by a machine which tests its strength, it is

....

17.3 Complete the article about the environmental considerations of wood using words from B and C opposite.

From an environmental perspective, wood has many advantages. Firstly, it comes from a sustainable source. Coniferous trees grow relatively fast, providing a rapidly replaceable source of (1) .... Secondly, almost all the timber in a tree can be utilized, leaving little or no waste. The best quality wood can be used for structural applications, where solid, (2) .... sections are required by engineers; for high-strength elements such as (3) .... beams; and in the high-quality plies used to make (4) .... Smaller strands can be made into engineering wood with structural properties, such as (5) .... And small particles and fibres, including those from waste timber, can go into cheaper materials, like (6) .... board and (7) ....

Glue-laminated timber in the Scottish Parliament building in Edinburgh, Scotland

Over to you

What types of timber are used in your home and/or office, both as building materials and to make fixtures and furniture within the building?

18 Material properties 1

A ## Tensile strength and deformation

When materials are exposed to forces, such as **tension** (stretching forces ←□→) and **compression** (crushing forces →□←), they **deform** – that is, they change shape. The type of **deformation** depends on the type of force that is applied.

When a material is subjected to tension, its length will increase by a certain amount. This is called **extension** or **elongation**. It is especially important to understand the performance of materials **in tension**, as their **tensile strength** (ability to resist tension) is usually lower than their **compressive strength** (ability to resist compression).

B ## Elasticity and plasticity

Some materials can extend significantly, but still return to their original shape. A material's ability to do this is called **elasticity**. Rubber is an example of a very **elastic** material – it can be **elastically deformed** to a considerable extent.

If a material has very low elasticity, and is strong, engineers say it is **stiff**. If a material has low elasticity and is weak, it is described as **brittle** – that is, it **fractures** (breaks, due to tension) very easily. Glass is an example of a brittle material.

Some materials can change shape significantly, but do not return to their original shape. We say these materials are **plastic**. Often, **plasticity** is described in specific terms. A material that can be **plastically deformed** by hammering or rolling – for example, lead (Pb) – is **malleable**. A material that can be drawn out (stretched) into a long length – for example, copper (Cu) – is **ductile**.

C ## Stages in elastic and plastic deformation

The graph below shows the typical extension behaviour of ductile materials in **tensile testing** – where a sample bar is subjected to a progressively increasing tensile force.

Points 0–1 The extension of the bar is **proportional to** the increase in tension. For example, when tension increases by 10%, length increases by 10%.

Point 1 The bar reaches the **limit of proportionality**. Beyond this point, length begins to increase at a slightly greater rate than tension.

Point 2 The **elastic limit** is reached. Beyond this point, the bar will no longer return to its original length. In many materials, the elastic limit occurs almost immediately after the limit of proportionality.

Point 3 The bar reaches its **yield point**. Once it **yields**, it continues to increase in length, even without a further increase in tension.

Point 4 This is the **ultimate tensile strength** (**UTS**) of the material. Beyond this point, a **waist** (a narrower section) appears at a point along the length of the bar, signalling that it is about to fracture.

Point 5 This is the **fracture point**, where the bar breaks in two.

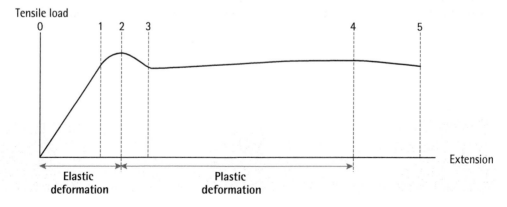

18.1 Complete the sentences using the words in the box. You will need to use one word twice. Look at A opposite to help you.

compression	deformation	elongation	extension	tension

1 A stretching force is called ....
2 A crushing force is called ....
3 Extension is also called ....
4 Tension causes .... or ....
5 Tension or compression cause ....

18.2 Match the two parts to make correct sentences. Look at B and C opposite to help you.

1 If a material is stiff
2 If a material is brittle
3 If a material is plastic
4 If a material yields
5 If a material fractures
6 If a material is elastically deformed

a it is malleable and/or ductile.
b it has low elasticity and low tensile strength.
c it has low elasticity and high tensile strength.
d it has been extended to a point before its elastic limit.
e it has been loaded beyond its ultimate tensile strength.
f it has been significantly plastically deformed, but not broken.

18.3 Complete the magazine article about springs using words from A, B and C opposite.

How are the springs used in car suspension made springy? It sounds like a silly question, but think about it for a moment. In order for a spring to compress or extend, then return to its original shape, it must be (1) ....
But springs are made from wire, and wire is made from very (2) .... metal (often cold drawn carbon steel). When the wire is manufactured, it is not only stretched beyond its (3) .... – meaning it will no longer return to its original length – but also beyond its (4) .... , where significant, irreversible (5) .... occurs.
The metal from which springs are made has therefore been (6) .... deformed and, consequently, needs to have its springiness put back.

To do this, once a spring has been formed into a coil, it is tempered – a process in which it is heated and kept at a high temperature for a sustained period. This 'resets' the atomic structure of the metal (partly, at least), so that after tempering, the spring will behave as it should – it can be (7) .... deformed and will subsequently return to its original shape.

Over to you

Think about a device, vehicle or structure you're familiar with, and the materials used to make it. What properties do the materials have? Which properties are strengths in this situation? Which properties are weaknesses, and how are these weaknesses overcome?

19 Material properties 2

A Hardness

The **hardness** of a material affects its **durability** – that is, how long it will last. Generally, **hard** materials are more **durable** than **soft** materials, because they are better at resisting **wear** – progressively worsening damage – to their surfaces. Hardness can be defined in two main ways:

- **Scratch hardness** describes a material's ability to resist being **scratched**. Materials with a high degree of scratch hardness are said to have good **abrasion resistance** – they are good at resisting damage due to **abrasion** (the action of two surfaces being rubbed together).

- **Indentation hardness** describes a material's ability to resist **indentations** – that is, compressions in the surface of a material caused by impacts.

Scratches

Indentations

B Fatigue, fracture toughness and creep

The article below is from an aviation magazine.

In aircraft construction, special attention must be paid to two materials problems that are well understood by mechanical and structural engineers.

One is **fatigue**, often called **metal fatigue** in metals. This problem is caused by **cyclic loads** – forces that continually vary. In aircraft, the wings are affected by cyclic loading as they frequently **flex**, continually bending up and down due to air turbulence. The consequence of fatigue is **micro-cracking** – the formation of cracks too small to see with the eye, and which worsen over time. The speed at which **fatigue cracking** progresses depends on the material's **fracture toughness**. This is a measure of how easily cracks that have already formed continue to open up and increase in length.

Another problem is **creep** - where components become permanently deformed (stretched, for example), due to loads. Creep increases over time. The problem is made worse by heat, so is a major issue in engines, where both loads and temperatures are high.

C Basic thermal properties

Some materials **conduct** (carry or transmit) heat better than others. Therefore, **thermal conductivity** varies, depending on the material. Copper, for example, is an excellent **thermal conductor**. Polystyrene, on the other hand, is an excellent **thermal insulator** (and so a very poor thermal conductor).

As temperature increases, most materials **expand** (increase in size due to heating), and as temperature falls, they **contract** (decrease in size due to cooling). The extent to which **expansion** and **contraction** occur is measured by a material's **coefficient of thermal expansion** – that is, its change in size for a given change in temperature. The coefficient for aluminium, for example, is 0.000023. This means that for an increase in temperature of one degree Celsius, a one-metre length of aluminium will increase in length by 0.000023 metres. This figure can also be referred to as the **coefficient of linear expansion**, since it describes change in length (a linear measurement).

19.1 Complete the design brief for part of a cutting machine using four of the words in the box. Look at A opposite to help you.

| abrasion | durability | durable | hard | indentation | scratch | soft |

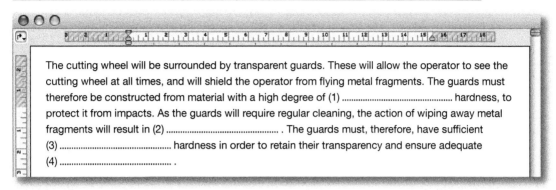

The cutting wheel will be surrounded by transparent guards. These will allow the operator to see the cutting wheel at all times, and will shield the operator from flying metal fragments. The guards must therefore be constructed from material with a high degree of (1) .... hardness, to protect it from impacts. As the guards will require regular cleaning, the action of wiping away metal fragments will result in (2) .... The guards must, therefore, have sufficient (3) .... hardness in order to retain their transparency and ensure adequate (4) ....

19.2 Match the descriptions (1–4) to the technical terms (a–d). Look at B opposite to help you.

1 the cause of fatigue
2 the consequence of fatigue
3 a material property that helps to slow down cracking
4 permanent changes in shape due to the action of loads over time

a creep
b cyclic loads
c micro-cracking
d fracture toughness

19.3 Complete the extract from an electrical design handbook using words and expressions from C opposite.

When comparing copper and aluminium as materials for electrical wires, it is necessary to consider their thermal properties. For instance, in situations where high temperatures are involved, it is important to understand how quickly wires (1) .... heat along their length – for example, away from hot parts, such as motors, towards heat-sensitive electrical components. In this regard, the (2) .... of copper is roughly 40% greater than that of aluminium, so copper is a much more effective (3) .... In the example above, a designer might therefore prefer aluminium wiring over copper wiring.

Another issue is thermal movement – the extent to which the metals (4) .... when heated, and (5) .... as they cool. In situations where temperature continually rises and falls, the resulting (6) .... and (7) .... can be problematic, as it can cause mechanical electrical connections to loosen over time. In this regard, copper has a (8) .... approximately 40% lower than that of aluminium. Copper therefore has the advantage in this respect, as it is less susceptible to movement.

Over to you

For a product you know about, say what the designer needed to consider with regard to:

■ abrasion   ■ indentations   ■ fatigue   ■ creep   ■ thermal issues.

What materials were chosen as a result of these considerations?

20 Forming, working and heat-treating metal

A Casting, sintering and extruding metal

Metal can be **formed** into shapes using heat and pressure. **Casting** involves heating metal until it becomes **molten** (liquid) and pouring it, or forcing it under pressure, into a mould called a **die**. Instead of being **cast**, metal components can be formed by **sintering**. This is done by using metal powder instead of molten metal. The powder is placed in a die and compressed into a solid mass. It is then heated (though not melted) until it becomes **sintered** – that is, the powder particles join together structurally, due to the heat.

Metal can also be shaped by **extruding** it into long lengths. **Extrusion** involves heating metal until it is molten, then forcing it at high pressure through a shaping tool – also called a die – to form bars or tubes, for example. At the same time, the metal cools and becomes solid.

B Working metal

Traditionally, many metal tools were made by heating iron bars in a fire, called a **forge**, until they were **red hot** or (hotter still) **white hot**. The metal was then **worked** – in other words, shaped by hammering it. **Working metal** using compression (for example, hammering) is also called **forging**. The same basic technique is still in use today, especially with steel. However, large, automated machines are now used. Metal is often worked (or **forged**) when hot (**hot forged**), but may also be worked when it is cold (**cold forged**).

A common forging technique is **drop forging**, where a heavy hammer is dropped onto a piece of metal. A die fixed to the hammer compresses the metal into the required shape. Rollers can also be used to apply compression, with or without heat, to produce **hot rolled** or **cold rolled** metal.

Forging also increases the hardness of metal. This is called **work hardening**. Metal becomes **work hardened** because its structure is changed by compression. The same result can be achieved without hammering or rolling – and therefore without changing the component's shape – by **shot-peening**. This involves firing small metal balls (metal shot) at the surface of components (when cold), at high speed. After components have been **shot-peened**, their surface is significantly harder.

Drop forged steel

C Heat treating metal

The properties of a metal can be changed by **heat treating** it – that is, heating and cooling the metal. The table below, from the technical information section of a steel supplier's website, summarizes the main types of **heat treatment**.

Type of heat treatment	Description of process	Properties of treated metal
quenching	Metal is heated, then dipped in water or oil to cool it rapidly.	**Quenched** metal is harder, but tends to be more brittle.
annealing	Metal is heated, then allowed to cool slowly.	**Annealed** metal is generally softer and more elastic.
tempering	Metal is heated and kept at a high temperature for a period of time.	**Tempered** metal possesses a balance between hardness and elasticity.
precipitation hardening (also called **age hardening**)	A process similar to tempering, but heat is maintained for longer.	**Precipitation-hardened** metal is harder than tempered metal.
case hardening (also called **surface hardening**)	Metal is heated in specific types of gas (not in air), causing its surface to absorb elements such as carbon.	Only the outer surface of **case-hardened** metal becomes harder.

20.1 Tick what is usually required in the metal forming processes (1–3). Look at A opposite to help you.

	molten metal	metal powder	heat	pressure	a die
1 casting	☐	☐	☐	☐	☐
2 sintering	☐	☐	☐	☐	☐
3 extrusion	☐	☐	☐	☐	☐

20.2 Decide whether the sentences below are true or false, and correct the false sentences. Look at B opposite to help you.

1 Metal must always be heated before it can be forged.
2 When referring to metals, the terms *working* and *forging* mean the same.
3 A common reason for forging metal is to increase its hardness.
4 One way of forging metal is by heating it and then rolling it.
5 Metal can only be rolled after it has been heated to a high temperature.
6 When metal is drop forged, it is subjected to compression.
7 Metal can only be work hardened by the process of hot forging.
8 Shot-peening is a hot forging technique used to work harden metal.

20.3 Make correct sentences using one part from each column. Look at C opposite to help you. The first one has been done for you.

1 If a metal is precipitation hardened,	it is held at a high temperature for a time,	making it harder, but more brittle.
2 When metal is annealed,	it is heated within a gas	to improve its hardness without reducing its elasticity too much.
3 If metal is quenched, this means	it can also be described as age hardened,	to harden only the metal near the surface.
4 When a metal is tempered,	its temperature is allowed to decrease gradually	because it is heated for a long time.
5 If a metal case is hardened,	its temperature is reduced rapidly,	in order to make it more elastic and less brittle.

20.4 Replace the highlighted expressions in the report extract with alternative words and expressions from A, B and C opposite. Sometimes there is more than one possible answer.

> The first stage in manufacturing the blades for the cutting tools is to form them into an approximate shape by (1) a process of squeezing molten metal through a die. Before the blades have cooled, they are then (2) hammered while still at a high temperature – a process which not only flattens them into their final shape, but also ensures the metal becomes (3) harder as a result of the hammering action. The blades are then (4) cooled quickly in water. Finally, they are (5) bombarded with small metal balls in order to further increase their surface hardness.

Over to you

Think of a type of steel component that needs to have specific properties. Suggest different ways of obtaining these properties by forging or heat treating the steel.

Raw materials for processing

Generally, **raw materials** are materials which need to be processed before they are used – for example, melted and cast in a mould. Common formats of raw material are:

- **powder**: quantities of very **fine** (small) **particles**, such as cement powder
- **pellets**: larger, standard-sized pieces of material, typically pea-sized to egg-sized, intended to be melted for forming in moulds – for instance, plastic pellets
- **fibres**: very fine, hair-like lengths, such as glass fibres.

When steel and other metals are produced, they are made into blocks called **ingots**, which can subsequently be melted and cast. Very large steel ingots are called **blooms**. One standard size for steel blooms is 630 mm x 400 mm x 6 m. Steel can also be supplied in smaller blocks, of various sizes, called **billets**.

Formats of processed materials

Materials are frequently supplied ready for use in the formats described below.

- **Bars** are long lengths of solid metal with a relatively small cross-sectional area. These can be **round bars** (or **rods**) which have a circular section. They may also be **square bars**, with a square section, and **flat bars**, with a flat, rectangular section. A bar is generally made of metal, but a rod can be made of any material.

- **Sheets** are flat, wide and thin – for steel, thinner than about 3 mm. Other materials supplied in sheets include plastic, glass and wood. However, sheets of wood are often called **boards**. When **sheets of metal** (or **metal sheets**) are delivered in large quantities, they can be supplied in rolls called **coils**.

- **Plates** are flat pieces of metal that are wide, but thicker than sheets (for steel, thicker than 3 mm). Non-metals, such as glass, plastic or wood, are not usually called plates; even if these materials are thicker than 3 mm, they are usually called sheets.

- **Structural steel sections** are made from rolled or extruded steel, and produced in a variety of section shapes. **I-sections**, with profiles in the shape of the letter *I*, are common examples. (See Appendix V on page 106 for types of structural section.)

- **Tubes** are **hollow**, not solid. The most common types are **round tubes**, but **square tubes** and **rectangular tubes** are also produced. **Pipes** are specifically for carrying liquid or gas. A pipe is therefore just one type of tube.

- **Wires** are thin lengths of metal with circular sections, consisting of one **strand** – that is, a long, thin, single piece of material. They are usually supplied in coils. Several wires can be combined to form a **cable**. An **electrical wire** is a single conductor covered with insulation. The conductor can be a single wire (called a **solid wire**) or several strands of wire grouped together (called a **stranded wire**). An **electrical cable** has several conductors, separately covered with insulation, grouped within a second outer layer of insulation.

Electrical cable with solid wires

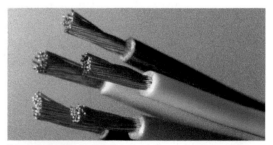

Stranded wires

Note: **Tubes** can also be called **tubing** – for example, **steel tubing**.

21.1 Decide whether the sentences below are true or false, and correct the false sentences. Look at A opposite to help you.

1 Raw materials are often intended to be melted or mixed.
2 Powder particles are smaller than pellets.
3 Pellets do not require further processing.
4 A steel bloom is a type of ingot.
5 Steel billets can be cut into smaller sized pieces called blooms.

21.2 Complete the descriptions below the photos using the words in the box. You will need to use some words more than once. Look at B opposite to help you.

bar	cable	flat	rod	sheet	stranded	wire
bloom	coil	plate	round	solid	tube	

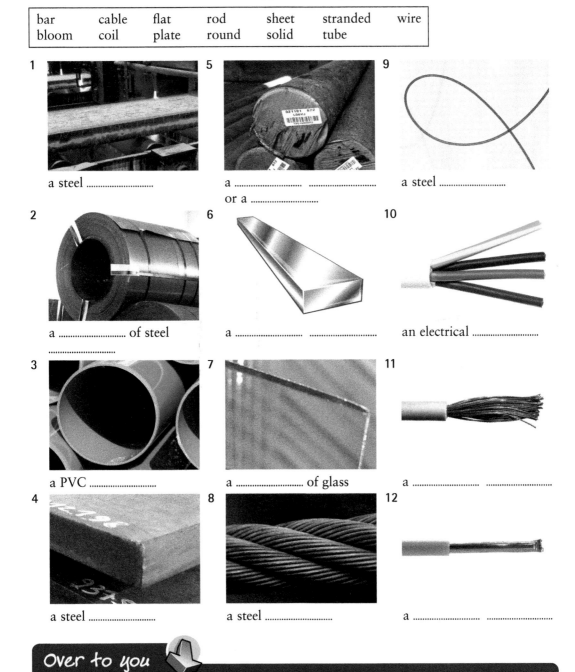

1 a steel ....

2 a .... of steel ....

3 a PVC ....

4 a steel ....

5 a .... or a ....

6 a ....

7 a .... of glass

8 a steel ....

9 a steel ....

10 an electrical ....

11 a ....

12 a ....

Over to you

Think about the individual components in a device, installation or structure you know about. In what form do you think the material used for each component was supplied?

22 3D component features

A 3D forms of edges and joints

The plan and sections below show the end of a stainless steel pipe and an access plate, which are part of a production line at a chemicals manufacturing plant.

The top edge of the plate is **chamfered** – at an angle of 45 degrees with the sides of the plate. All the other edges are **square** (90 degrees). Around the bottom of the plate is a **rebate** – an internal corner. The top of the pipe is also **rebated** around the inside, so that the bottom of the plate can **slot into** the top of the pipe.

In the rebate on the pipe, there is a **ridge** – a long, thin, raised surface. On the plate, a **groove** or **channel** is cut into the metal. The ridge on the pipe slots into this groove to form a **tongue-and-groove joint** (the ridge is the **tongue**). When the two are slotted together there is a **cavity** or **void** (a hollow space) between the top of the tongue and the end of the groove. This is to **accommodate** (provide a space for) a rubber sealing ring.

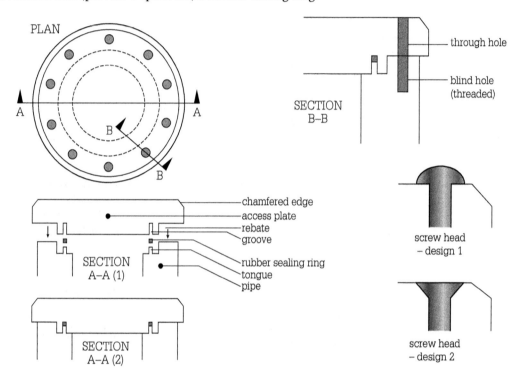

B 3D forms of holes and fasteners

■ The holes in the plate, for screws, are **through holes** – they go through the metal. The holes in the pipe wall are **blind holes** – they do not go all the way through. The screws which are intended to be **screwed into** these holes (by a turning action) have **threads** (helical grooves). The internal surfaces of the holes in the pipe walls are also **threaded**.

■ The screws are machine screws, which have a **constant** thickness – their thickness is the same along their length. Many other screws are **tapered** – their thickness decreases towards the **tip** of the screw (the narrower end). Many screws are also **pointed** – the thickness of their tip reduces to zero.

■ Two design options are shown for the screw heads. In Design 1, the screw has a **round head**, which is **raised** or **proud** – it is at a higher level than the surface of the plate. In Design 2, the screw has a **flat head** and is fully **recessed** – the head is within the thickness of the plate. The head is **flush with** (at the same level as) the top of the plate. To make the screw heads **flush**, the top of the hole and the sides of the screw head are chamfered. Recessing screws in this way is called **countersinking** – the screws are **countersunk**.

22.1 The extracts below are from technical conversations about machine tools. Match the pairs of sentences and choose the correct word from the brackets in the second sentence. Look at A and B opposite to help you.

1 According to the drawing, we cut to a depth of 40 mm in a 60 mm thick plate.
2 The edge of the die is cut off at 45 degrees.
3 The tool is used as a scribe for scratching lines on the surfaces of ceramics.
4 It's important to ensure the joint fits together properly.
5 The surface needs to be flat.

a So the inside of the (groove/tongue) must be perfectly smooth.
b So the screw heads must be (raised/flush).
c It's a (blind/through) hole.
d That's why the end is (rounded/pointed), to make it sharp.
e It's (chamfered/rebated).

22.2 Complete the description of a screwdriver and screw using the words in the box. Look at A and B opposite to help you.

accommodate	constant	flush	recessed	rounded	square	threaded
chamfered	countersunk	groove	ridge	slot	tapered	tip

The end of the screwdriver is (1) ...., progressively reducing in thickness towards its (2) .... This allows it to fit a range of different sized screw heads.

The screw has a flat head. Running across the centre of the head is a (3) ...., which has (4) .... edges. This is designed to (5) .... screwdrivers, which (6) .... into it.

The top edge of the screw head is (7) .... This avoids having a sharp edge, which could cause cuts.

The tapered side of the head allows the screw to be (8) .... The advantage of this is that the screw head can be fully (9) .... within the material surrounding the screw, making the screw head (10) .... with the surface of the material.

The top part of the screw shaft is smooth and has a (11) .... diameter.

The lower part of the screw is (12) .... The close-up picture shows that the (13) .... forming the outer part of the thread is not pointed, but (14) ....

Over to you

Describe the 3D features of some components or assemblies you know about.

23 Machining 1

A Machining and CNC

Machining is the use of machines to cut pieces of material (called **workpieces**) and shape them into components. The tools used in machining, to make holes, grooves, threads, etc., are called **machine tools**. Metal is often **machined**. As it is cut, waste is produced, called **swarf** or **chips**. During machining, a liquid called **cutting fluid** may be pumped onto the workpiece to act as a **coolant**, keeping the workpiece cool.

In manufacturing, machining is usually guided by computers called **computer numerical control** (**CNC**) systems. Often, design information (on shapes and sizes of components) is fed directly into CNC systems from **computer aided design / computer aided manufacturing** (**CAD/CAM**) software.

Note: **CAD/CAM** is said as two words: /ˈkæd ˌkæm/.

B Machining with cutting tools

Below are the most common machining techniques which use cutting tools.

Milling is cutting done by a **milling machine**, often using **toothed** cutting discs (wheels with **teeth** that have sharp edges). When a workpiece is **milled**, it is held in a fixed position on the machine, and is shaped by cutting tools which **rotate** (spin) while being moved over the surface of the workpiece.

Turning is a technique for cutting components that have a circular cross-section. The workpiece is **turned** by a machine called a **lathe**, which rotates the workpiece. A fixed machine tool is then moved against the rotating workpiece to cut material from it.

Turning using a lathe

A band saw

Sawing is cutting using a **blade** (a thin, sharp piece of metal), which usually has teeth, to remove a thickness of material slightly wider than the blade. The gap left by the blade, along the line of the cut, is called a **kerf**. Machines that use toothed blades include **circular saws**, which have rotating circular blades, **band saws**, and **power hacksaws**. A **hacksaw** has a blade with very small teeth, for cutting metal. Saws may also use **abrasive wheels** – that is, thin, circular cutting wheels with rough, hard surfaces – often made of industrial diamond.

Drilling is a technique for cutting circular holes. A machine called a **drill** is fitted with a tool called a **drill bit** (or **bit**). The bit rotates and **drills into** the material. Holes with large diameters can be cut using **holesaws** – hollow cylinders with teeth, which saw circular cuts and remove a **core** (a solid cylinder) of material. When used to drill into concrete, this technique is also called **core drilling**, or **diamond drilling**, as the holesaws have industrial diamond edges. Usually, drilling refers to making new holes. In machining, **enlarging** a hole (making it wider) is called **boring**.

Grinding is removing material across a surface area, using abrasive wheels. The machines used to **grind** materials with abrasive wheels are called **grinders**.

23.1 Match the two parts to make correct sentences. Look at A and B opposite to help you.

1 A drill bit is an example of
2 Material being machined is called
3 The waste metal produced during machining is called
4 Metal gets hot during cutting, so cutting fluid can be used as
5 A computer that guides a machining process is called
6 Drawings can be produced and transferred to the machining process using

a CAD/CAM software.
b a CNC system.
c a machine tool.
d a workpiece.
e swarf or chips.
f a coolant.

23.2 Complete the descriptions below the photos using the words in the box. Look at B opposite to help you.

abrasive	blade	cores	drill	grinder	holesaw	toothed
bit	circular	diamond	drilling	hacksaw	saw	wheel

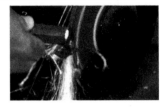

1 a ....   3 a .... for a   5 a thick ....
   for metal   .... on a ....

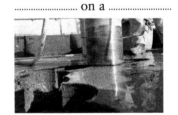

2 a ....   4 a .... blade for a   6 .... of concrete
                                    ....   being removed by
                                                              ....

23.3 Complete the sentences using the words in the box. Look at B opposite to help you.

drill	grind	mill	turn	saw

1 Lathes are designed to .... workpieces.
2 Different bits are designed to .... into different types of material.
3 When you .... a workpiece, the cutting blade removes a thickness of material to form a kerf.
4 Abrasive wheels .... material.
5 On some machines, toothed cutting wheels can be used to .... any part of a workpiece, in order to form its final shape.

Over to you

Think about a specific metal component made by machining. What machine tools and machining techniques do you think were used to make it?

Machining 2

A Guillotining and punching

Thin materials can be cut by applying pressure in order to **shear** them – that is, cut them with a scissoring force (in engineering, called a **shear force**). Sheets of metal can be sheared using a machine called a **guillotine**, which has a long blade. Usually, sheets are **guillotined** when long, straight cuts are required.

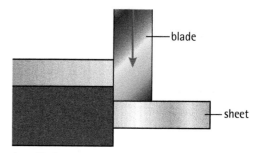

A guillotine

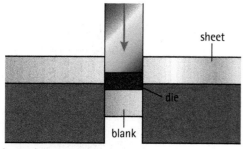

A punch

Small shapes, such as circles, can be sheared from sheets using a machine called a **punch**, which pushes a **die** (a shaped tool) through the sheet. The shaped piece of metal that is **punched** from the sheet is called a **blank**. If the blank is the finished product, this process is called **blanking**. If the sheet itself, with holes made in it, is the finished product, the process is called **piercing**.

B High-temperature metal cutting techniques

Flame-cutting generally uses oxygen (O_2) and acetylene (C_2H_2). The two gases are blown through a **torch** – basically a tube – as a mixture called **oxyacetylene**. The acetylene burns in the oxygen to produce a flame hot enough to melt steel.

Electrical discharge machining (**EDM**) – also called **spark erosion** – involves passing a tight length of wire through a workpiece, similar to the way thin wire is used to cut cheese. However, the wire does not actually touch the workpiece. Instead, a high-voltage current produces an **electric arc**, which 'jumps' across a small gap between the wire and the workpiece. As the current **arcs**, it generates heat, which melts the metal ahead of the wire.

Plasma cutting uses a **plasma torch** to blow out gas at high pressure. The gas argon (Ar) is often used. At the same time a high-voltage current is passed through the plasma torch, and arcs between the torch and the workpiece. This **ionizes** some of the atoms in the gas, changing it to **plasma**. As the plasma is heated by the arc, it reaches an extremely high temperature – much hotter than would be possible for a gas that had not been ionized.

Note: When atoms are **ionized**, their **electrons** – tiny negatively charged particles that are normally attached to the atom – break away and float freely within the gas.

C Laser cutting and UHP waterjets

Laser beams (concentrated light) can cut materials accurately, in small quantities, by melting them. **Laser cutting** is especially suitable for plastics.

Ultra-high-pressure (**UHP**) **waterjets** – jets of water fired at extremely high pressure – can cut almost any material, including metal. An advantage of **UHP waterjet cutting** is that the **edge quality** of workpieces is high – that is, the cut edges are smooth. This means that no **secondary operations** – further processes to smooth rough edges – are required. Also, because UHP waterjets are cold, they do not leave a **heat-affected zone** (**HAZ**) on the workpiece – that is, an area near the cut edge whose properties have been changed by heat.

24.1 Match the cutting processes (1–4) to the descriptions (a–e). You will need to use some of the descriptions more than once. Look at A opposite to help you.

1 blanking
2 guillotining
3 piercing
4 punching

a shearing material
b applying pressure to a blade to make long, straight cuts
c applying pressure to a die to make small, shaped (not straight) cuts
d applying pressure to a die to produce workpieces with holes in them
e applying pressure to a die to cut small, shaped workpieces from sheets

24.2 Complete the descriptions of the photos using words from B and C opposite.

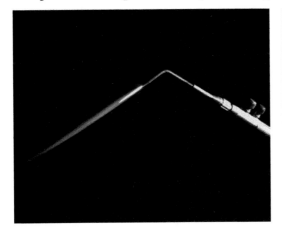

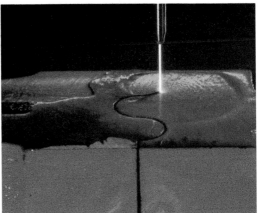

This torch burns (1) .... (C_2H_2) in a flow of (2) .... – a mixture called (3) .... The torch can be used for (4) ....-.............................. .

This machine is used for (5) ..............................-..............................-.............................. waterjet cutting. It produces workpieces with very smooth edges. Because of this high (6) .... , the workpiece does not need to be put through (7) .... in order to smooth its edges.

24.3 Answer the questions below, about non-mechanical machining techniques. Look at B and C opposite to help you.

1 In machining, what does EDM stand for?
2 What alternative term can be used instead of EDM?
3 What type of tool is used in both flame-cutting and plasma cutting?
4 What source of heat is used in both EDM and plasma cutting?
5 What needs to happen to a gas in order to turn it into plasma?
6 What term refers to concentrated light that can be hot enough to cut material?
7 What term refers to an area of material that has been changed by high temperature?

Over to you

Give examples of different components, made of different materials, that could be cut using some of the techniques described opposite. Say why the cutting technique would be especially suitable for the component and for the material.

25 Interconnection

A Attaching and supporting

The individual components that make up assemblies and structures can be **connected** (or **connected together**) in different ways. The pictures below show an example: a **connection** (or **joint**) between a steel column and a concrete foundation.

The foundation **supports** the column, preventing downward movement. As well as **providing support**, it **anchors** the column, holding it in position to stop it sliding or lifting. To provide a connection, bolts are **attached to** a plate at the bottom of the column – called a **base plate**. The bottoms of the bolts are **embedded in** the concrete of the foundation – that is, they are surrounded and held by the concrete.

A and B are	attached. connected. joined.	
	attached connected fastened fixed held joined	together.
A is	attached connected fastened fixed joined	to B.

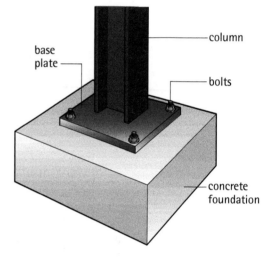

column
base plate
bolts
concrete foundation

B Fitting together

When foundations for steel columns are poured, cone-shaped holes are formed in the concrete to accommodate bolts to hold down the base plate. The holes allow the tops of the bolts to have a certain amount of **play** – that is, they are free to move slightly. This means the bolts can be **adjusted** (moved as required) to allow the bolts to **slot through** the holes in the base plate, so that the plate and bolts can **fit together**.

As the column is lowered into position, steel wedges are placed below the base plate. These act as **packers** (also called **spacers** or **shims**), and leave a **gap** (narrow space) between the plate and the concrete. The wedges also enable **adjustments** to be made. By hammering a wedge horizontally, the side of the base plate can be lifted, allowing the column to be plumbed (made exactly vertical).

A type of cement, called grout, is then placed beneath the base plate. This **fills** the gap between the base plate and the foundation, and the holes around the bolts. It also **seals** the joint against rainwater, protecting the bolts from corrosion.

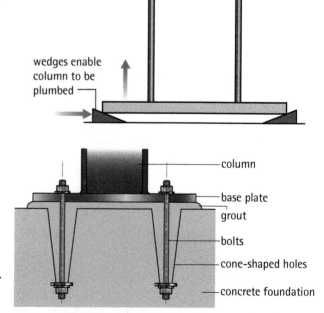

wedges enable column to be plumbed

column
base plate
grout
bolts
cone-shaped holes
concrete foundation

Section at column base

25.1 Complete the description of parts of a suspension bridge using the correct forms of words from A opposite. Sometimes there is more than one possible answer.

Photo 1

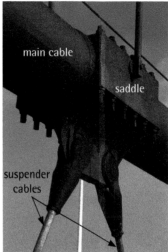

Photo 2

Photo 1 shows a suspension bridge. The bridge's two main cables are (1) .... by towers. The cables are (2) .... at each end by huge blocks of concrete, which are deeply (3) .... in the ground.

Photo 2 shows a (4) .... between one of the bridge's main cables, and two smaller suspender cables. The suspender cables are (5) .... to the main cable by a component called a saddle. The saddle is made up of two parts that are fixed (6) .... by bolts. The many wires which make up the main cable are covered by a protective layer of very thin wire that is wrapped around the main cable in the form of a helix (the shape of a spring).

25.2 Match the two parts of the sentences about possible technical issues during the installation of cable saddles on a new suspension bridge. Look at B opposite to help you.

1 These bolts are slightly too thick, so
2 Some of the saddles don't fit tightly enough – there's a slight gap between the saddle and the cable, so
3 The holes in the top of this saddle don't line up exactly with the holes in the bottom part, so
4 The wire that's wrapped around the outside of the main cable isn't sealed against the edge of some of the saddles, so
5 The saddles are all different – they're manufactured to correspond with the angle of the main cable at the point where they're fixed, so

a they won't fit together properly.
b the joints aren't properly protected against rainwater.
c they're not designed for adjustment.
d they won't slot through the holes in the saddles.
e even when they're fully tightened there's too much play.

Over to you

Think of a device or structure you're familiar with. Describe how it fits together, and how different components are fixed and/or supported.

A Bolts

The photo below shows a common **fastener** (or **fixing**): a **bolt**, with a **nut**. Bolts have **threads** – grooves on the outside of the bolt's **shaft** (or **shank**), which run around the shaft in a **helical** pattern. The **threaded** shaft allows a nut, which has a thread inside it, to be **screwed onto** the bolt (by a turning motion). Nuts usually have a **right-hand thread** – they are **screwed on** by turning them **clockwise** (in the direction of clock hands) and **unscrewed** by turning them **anticlockwise**. However, in some situations, **left-hand threads** are used.

Most bolts have **heads** with hexagonal perimeters (**hexagonal heads** or **hex heads**). These allow a **spanner** to turn them. Heads can also have a hexagonal hole in their top, called a **socket head**. This allows a **hex key** (or **Allen key**) to fit into them.

thread
shaft or shank
head
A nut   A bolt

A spanner

A hex key or Allen key

Note: A nut is **screwed onto** a bolt;
a bolt can be **screwed into** a threaded hole.

BrE: anticlockwise; AmE: counterclockwise
BrE: spanner; AmE: wrench

B Preload in bolted joints

Turning force, called **torque**, is applied to bolts to **tighten** them – that is, to make them grip tightly. As a bolt is tightened, the **tension** (stretching force) in its shaft increases, and the components being **bolted together** are pressed tightly together. This pressing force is called **preload** (or **clamp load**). If enough preload is applied, friction between the components will prevent them sliding in different directions. This is an advantage, as sliding subjects the sides of bolts to **shear force** (scissoring force), which can cause them to break. In steel structures, bolts that apply high preloads to prevent sliding are called **high strength friction grip** (**HSFG**) bolts.

The amount of torque applied to bolts can be adjusted using a **torque wrench**, a tool which can tighten and **loosen** bolts, and which indicates how much torque is applied. This helps to ensure that bolts are tightened enough, but not **over-tightened**. Torque wrenches are also useful for checking that **bolted joints** do not **work loose** – that is, that they do not become loose over time.

Note: See Unit 31 for more on torque, tension, shear and other forces.

C Washers

Washers are metal discs which fit between the head of a bolt or a nut and the components being bolted together. Ordinary washers – called **flat washers** or **plain washers** – have a larger outside diameter than the bolt head or nut. Their wider area is intended to **spread the load** (distribute pressure) over the surface of the component as the bolt is tightened.

Spring washers are designed to be compressed, to allow the amount of preload to be adjusted as the bolt is tightened. In some situations, spring washers are used to allow a bolt to move slightly, in order to absorb shocks. Common types of spring washer are **helical spring washers** and **conical spring washers**.

A plain or flat washer

A helical spring washer

A conical spring washer

26.1 Change one word in each of the sentences below to make them correct. Look at A opposite to help you.

1 Wrenches are well-known examples of fasteners.
2 In most cases, nuts are screwed onto bolts by turning them anticlockwise.
3 The threaded part of a bolt is the head.
4 Threads are cut to form a hexagonal pattern.
5 Allen keys are designed to fit around the heads of bolts.

26.2 Use the words in the box to complete the text about bolted joints, taken from a bolt supplier's website. Look at B opposite to help you.

loosen	shear force	tighten	over-tighten
preload	tension	torque	work loose

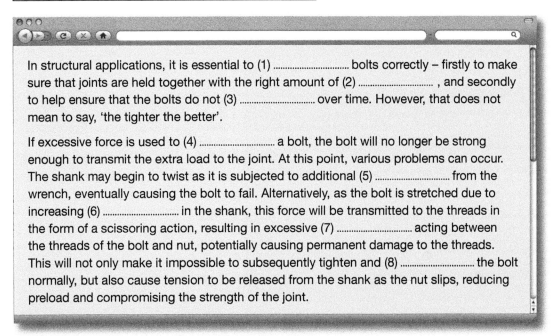

In structural applications, it is essential to (1) .... bolts correctly – firstly to make sure that joints are held together with the right amount of (2) .... , and secondly to help ensure that the bolts do not (3) .... over time. However, that does not mean to say, 'the tighter the better'.

If excessive force is used to (4) .... a bolt, the bolt will no longer be strong enough to transmit the extra load to the joint. At this point, various problems can occur. The shank may begin to twist as it is subjected to additional (5) .... from the wrench, eventually causing the bolt to fail. Alternatively, as the bolt is stretched due to increasing (6) .... in the shank, this force will be transmitted to the threads in the form of a scissoring action, resulting in excessive (7) .... acting between the threads of the bolt and nut, potentially causing permanent damage to the threads. This will not only make it impossible to subsequently tighten and (8) .... the bolt normally, but also cause tension to be released from the shank as the nut slips, reducing preload and compromising the strength of the joint.

26.3 Decide whether the sentences below are true or false, and correct the false sentences. Look at C opposite to help you.

1 The purpose of all washers is to spread the load from the bolt across the surfaces of the components being bolted together.
2 Plain washers are flat.
3 Spring washers change shape as a bolt is tightened.
4 Spring washers ensure that, no matter how much a bolt is tightened, the amount of preload remains the same.
5 In situations where components are subjected to shocks, spring washers ensure that no movement occurs between the bolt and the component.

Over to you

Think about a type of machine or structure you know about which has bolted joints. Answer the following questions about the technical characteristics of the joints:

● How accurately must preload be adjusted?

● Are the bolts designed to resist shear forces, or do they work as HSFG bolts?

● Are any types of washer used? What is their purpose?

A Screws

Screws have threaded shafts with heads. They may be screwed into a **predrilled** hole – drilled for the screw to enter. **Self-tapping screws** do not require predrilled holes. They cut their own hole as they are screwed in. Unlike bolts, screws are not used with nuts and – generally – are not screwed into threaded holes. Most **screw heads** are designed to be **screwed in** using a **screwdriver**. The most common types are **slot head screws** and **crosshead screws**.

A screwdriver

A slot head screw

A crosshead screw, Phillips type

A crosshead screw, Pozidriv type

Small-diameter bolts, which can be used with nuts or screwed into threaded holes, are sometimes called **machine screws**. Bolts that hold components in place by pressing the end of the bolt against the component, in order to generate friction and prevent sliding, are called **set screws** or **grub screws**. Examples of uses are holding a wheel on a shaft, and connecting electric wires.

B Screw anchors

Fasteners designed to fix objects to walls are called **screw anchors**. These fit into predrilled holes. A simple screw anchor is a plastic tube called a **wall plug** (or **plug**). It is inserted in a hole, and a screw or bolt is then screwed into it. As it enters the plug, the plug **expands** (its diameter increases). This increases friction, allowing the plug to resist **pullout forces** – the forces which would cause it to be pulled out of the hole if it were not firmly **anchored**. An **expansion anchor** is another type of anchor. It consists of a bolt fitted inside a metal sleeve. The sleeve expands as the bolt is tightened in the hole.

In cases where pullout forces are very high, **chemical anchors** can be used. These are **studs** – threaded bars, onto which nuts can be screwed. The studs are **set in** – that is, held in the hole by an adhesive. Most chemical anchors are **set into** holes using a strong adhesive called epoxy resin (see Unit 29 for more on adhesives).

C Rivets

Rivets are permanent fasteners – they cannot be unscrewed. A **solid rivet** consists of a short, solid shaft of metal with a head at one end, called the **factory head**. The rivet is inserted through a pre-drilled hole, then a special tool is used to **deform** (change the shape of) the other end of the rivet, flattening and widening it to form a second head, called the **shop head**. Solid rivets are widely used in aircraft.

Blind rivets (or **pop rivets**) are made from hollow tubes, and are fitted using a tool called a **rivet gun**. Blind rivets are not suitable for high-strength joints.

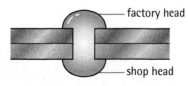
factory head
shop head
A cross-section of a solid rivet

A blind rivet

Solid rivets after installation

27.1 Make word combinations with *screw* using words from A and B opposite. Then match the combinations with the descriptions (1–5) below. One description can be used twice.

1 A .... screw is a thin bolt.
2 A .... screw does not require a predrilled hole.
3 A .... screw has a straight groove cut into the top.
4 A .... screw fits screwdrivers with an X-shaped profile at the end.
5 A .... screw applies pressure at its end to hold a component in place.

27.2 Complete the article from a home improvements magazine using the words in the box. Look at A and B opposite to help you.

crosshead	expand	head	plug	pullout	screw	screwdriver	set in

How **NOT** to use wall plugs ...

You check the diameter of hole required, then choose a drill bit one millimetre narrower. You've tried drilling the specified hole size many times in the past, only for it to be too big, leaving the (1) ....
spinning in the hole when you try to tighten the (2) .... You decide it's better to ensure a tight fit. So you drill a smaller hole than suggested, then attempt to hammer in the plug. It bends sideways, useless. You try again. And again. Eventually, you manage to get a plug into the hole. You insert the end of the screw, pick up your (3) .... and get to work. It certainly is a tight fit. And hard work. And as the screw goes in, and the plug starts to (4) ...., the going gets harder.
By the time the screw's halfway in, the screwdriver has slipped off the screw so many times that what used to be a (5) .... pattern on the screw (6) ....
now looks more like a smooth, round hole. It's impossible to screw it in any further. Or unscrew it. So you take a pair of pliers, grip the end of the screw, and attempt to drag the whole thing out of the wall. But the (7) .... force is beyond the power of your now-aching arms. The screw might as well be (8) .... with epoxy resin.

27.3 Match the descriptions (1–5) to the terms (a–e). Look at C opposite to help you.

1 a type of fastener that is hollow
2 a type of fastener that is not hollow
3 a tool used for installing a type of fastener
4 the wide part at the top of a rivet, present when the rivet is supplied
5 the wide part at the bottom of a rivet, formed after the rivet is inserted

a rivet gun
b shop head
c factory head
d solid rivet
e blind rivet

Over to you

Think of an assembly or installation you know about, where screws are used as fasteners.
Say what types of screw are used, and suggest why each type was specified.

A Welding

Welding means permanently joining two pieces of material by heating the joint between them. The heat melts the edges of the components being **welded together,** and once the material has become **molten** (liquid), **fusion** occurs. When the joint **fuses,** material from each component is mixed together, joining to form a solid **weld.** Metal is often **welded.** It is also possible to weld plastic.

Welding is usually used to join components of the same **base metal** – that is, the metal the components are made of. It is possible – though more difficult – to weld certain **dissimilar materials.** For example, copper can be **welded to** steel. Often, a **filler** is added during welding. This is new material, of the same type as the base metal, which is melted into the **weld pool** – the molten metal at the joint during welding.

One problem in welding is **discontinuity,** where joints are not completely solid. Another problem is **residual stress.** This is force – for example, tension – which is 'trapped' around the joint. This problem occurs after welding, as a result of contraction in the **weld zone** (or **fusion zone**) – the area that was the weld pool. It can also occur in the **heat-affected zone** (**HAZ**) – the material close to the weld pool which was subjected to high temperature, and was modified by the heat.

B Common gas and arc welding techniques

Shielded metal arc welding (**SMAW**), generally called **arc welding** or **stick welding,** involves **striking an electric arc** between the workpiece and an **electrode** – an electrical conductor. The heat from the arc melts the base metal. The electrode consists of a **welding rod** – a stick of metal of the same type as the workpiece – which provides filler. The welding rod is therefore **consumable** – it is used up. The rod is also coated with a material called **flux.** When heated, this produces a **shielding gas,** which protects the molten metal from oxygen. Without this gas, the hot metal would combine with the oxygen in the air, and this would weaken the weld.

Shielded metal arc welding

In **gas welding,** heat comes from a torch which burns **oxyfuel** – a mixture of **oxygen** (O_2) and a gas fuel. The gas fuel burns much hotter in oxygen than it would in the air. The most common fuel is **acetylene** (C_2H_2) – called **oxyacetylene** when mixed with oxygen. Welding rods provide filler but flux is not required, as the burning oxyfuel produces **carbon dioxide** (CO_2) which acts as a shielding gas.

In **gas metal arc welding** (**GMAW**) – often called **MIG welding** (**Metal Inert Gas**) – an arc is struck between the workpiece and a wire which is made of the same metal as the base metal. The wire acts as a consumable

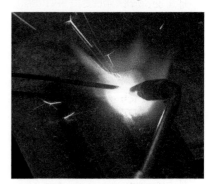
Gas welding using oxyacetylene

electrode, supplying filler. A shielding gas, often **argon** (Ar), is blown onto the weld pool.

In **gas tungsten arc welding** (**GTAW**) – often called **TIG welding** (**Tungsten Inert Gas**) – an arc comes from an electrode made of tungsten (W). However, the tungsten is **non-consumable** – it does not melt, and is not **consumed** as filler during the welding process. A separate welding rod is used to supply filler, if required. As with MIG welding, a shielding gas such as argon is blown onto the weld.

Note: **MIG** and **TIG** are said as words: /mɪg/ and /tɪg/.

28.1 Complete the extract from a technical document about welding using the words in the box. You will need to use some words twice. Look at A opposite to help you.

base	fuse	metal	residual	weld
discontinuities	heat-affected	molten	stresses	welded
dissimilar	materials	pool	together	zone

It is possible for components made of different metals to be (1) ....
.... For instance, steel can be welded to copper and to brass. However, it is
much more difficult to weld components made of two (2) ....
than it is to weld those made of the same (3) .... While there is
no difficulty in melting two different metals and mixing them together in a (4) ....
state, problems occur once the hot, liquid metal forming the (5) ....
.... starts to cool. As this process takes place, the two metals will not necessarily
(6) .... properly. Once the joint has cooled, this can result in (7) .... ,
such as cracks, at the heart of the (8) .... In addition, as the
metals contract at different rates (due to different coefficients of thermal expansion),
powerful (9) .... can build up, not only in the joint, but also in the
wider (10) .... near the joint.

28.2 Match the two parts to make eleven correct sentences about welding techniques. You will need to use some parts more than once. Look at B opposite to help you.

1 Shielded metal arc welding uses
2 Gas welding uses
3 Gas metal arc welding uses
4 Gas tungsten arc welding uses

a burning gas.
b a consumable electrode.
c a non-consumable electrode.
d a separate welding rod which is not an electrode.
e a special coating on the welding rod which produces a shielding gas.
f a separate gas supply, blown onto the weld as a shielding gas.
g a shielding gas generated by burned oxyfuel.
h a gas whose purpose is to increase the temperature of the welding process.

28.3 Match each of the substances (1–6) to the description (a–h) above that uses the substance. Look at B opposite to help you.

1 flux
2 argon
3 oxygen
4 tungsten
5 acetylene
6 carbon dioxide

Over to you

Think about the different techniques used for welding metals in the industry you work in, or in an industry you know about. In what specific situations are different techniques used, and why are they suitable?

A Specialized welding techniques

The web page below, from a technical guide to welding techniques, explains some more specialized welding methods.

Resistance welding involves passing an electric current through metal components that are touching. This heats the metal and welds it. The technique can be used for **spot welding** – welding a number of small points between the surfaces of the components. It can also be used for **seam welding**, to make long, narrow welds.

Ultrasonic welding uses high-frequency **acoustic vibrations** (sound vibrations) to make the touching surfaces of two components vibrate. This generates friction, heating them and fusing them. The technique is often used to weld plastics.

B Brazing and soldering

In **brazing**, brass – an alloy of copper (Cu) and zinc (Zn) – is melted using an oxyfuel torch, and added as filler to form the joint. Unlike welding, the base metal of the components is not melted, so the components are not fused. **Brazed** joints are therefore not as strong as welded joints.

For some pipe joints and for electrical connections, **soldering** is often used. **Solder** is a metal filler which melts at quite a low temperature. Like brazing, soldering forms joints without melting the base metal. **Soldered** joints are therefore weaker than welds, and also generally weaker than brazed joints. In **soft soldering**, an alloy – of tin (Sn) and lead (Pb), or of tin and copper – is melted using an electrically heated rod called a **soldering iron**. In **hard soldering**, a solder containing copper and silver (Ag) produces slightly stronger joints. The higher melting point of silver means a flame – usually from an oxyfuel torch – is used instead of a soldering iron.

Soft soldering

C Adhesives

Adhesive – called **glue** in everyday language – can be used to **bond** (permanently join) components together. Its purpose is to **adhere to** the surfaces being joined, to create a **bond** between them. Most adhesives are liquids, which can be **applied to** (put on) the surfaces that need to be **glued together**.

Adhesives can create **adhesion** between surfaces in two main ways. One is by allowing wet adhesive to be absorbed by the components. After drying and hardening, this forms a **mechanical bond**, as adhesive is anchored into each component's **substrate** (the material below the surface). Adhesion may also be created by a **chemical bond**, from a chemical reaction between the adhesive and the materials.

Many types of adhesive harden by drying. They contain a **solvent** – water or a liquid chemical – which gives a workable mixture. After the adhesive has been applied, the solvent **evaporates** – turns from a liquid to a gas – to leave solid adhesive. An example of this type is **polyvinyl adhesive** (**PVA**), a wood glue. Other types, such as **epoxy resins** (see Unit 14), are **two-part adhesives,** supplied as separate chemicals in two containers. When mixed and applied, the two parts react, then **cure** – harden due to a chemical reaction.

Contact adhesives must be applied to both components, then left to dry for a time before the surfaces are brought together. A bond then occurs when the surfaces touch.

29.1 Make word combinations with *welding* using words from A opposite. Then match the combinations with the descriptions (1–4) below.

....
.... ⟨ welding ⟩
....
....

1 components are joined by several small welded points
2 the weld is in the form of a very thin line
3 high-frequency vibrations are generated by sound, causing friction and subsequent fusion
4 both components are connected to an electrical supply in order to be joined by spot welding or seam welding

29.2 Tick one or more of the boxes to show which technique(s) each sentence applies to, or leave all three boxes empty if the sentence applies to none. Look at B opposite to help you.

	brazing	soft soldering	hard soldering
1 Copper is used in the filler material.	☐	☐	☐
2 A soldering iron is used to melt the filler.	☐	☐	☐
3 The filler material contains silver.	☐	☐	☐
4 The base metal is melted to fuse with the filler.	☐	☐	☐
5 Heat is provided by a flame, often from oxyfuel.	☐	☐	☐
6 Tin is used in the filler material.	☐	☐	☐
7 This produces stronger joints than welding.	☐	☐	☐

29.3 Choose the correct words from the brackets to complete the sentences about adhesives. Look at C opposite to help you.

1 Surfaces can be glued together by applying different types of (adhesive / adhesion).
2 When adhesive-covered surfaces touch, they (adhere to / apply to) each other.
3 If an adhesive reacts with the material which the components are made from, it forms a (chemical bond / mechanical bond) with the material.
4 An adhesive that is applied to the surfaces of both components, then allowed to dry before they are joined, is called a (contact adhesive / two-part adhesive).
5 In order to form an effective mechanical bond, an adhesive must be absorbed quite deeply into the (solvent / substrate) of the material.
6 When two-part adhesives are mixed, they react chemically, which enables them to (cure / evaporate) and form a hard, strong material.

A tube of adhesive

Over to you

Think about the adhesives used in assemblies you're familiar with. Use language from C opposite to explain how the adhesives are used, and how they work.

30 Load, stress and strain

A Load

When engineers design a machine or structure, they need to know what forces will **be exerted on** it (put pressure on it). In engineering, forces are called **loads**. Usually, several different loads will **act on** – apply force to – the components in a machine, or the **members** (parts) of a structure. A component or member which is designed to **carry** (or **bear**) **a load** is called a **load-bearing** component or member.

To predict what will happen when components are **loaded**, engineers calculate the **magnitude** (size) of each load, and also work out the direction of the load – for example, vertically downwards. Load is therefore a **vector quantity** (or **vector**) – that is, a measurement with both a magnitude and a direction. This is different to a **scalar quantity**, which has a magnitude only.

Note: See Appendix V on page 106 for more on types of load.

B Stress and strain

The extract below is from an engineering textbook.

In a test, a thick cable is used to pick up a heavy object. The cable stretches slightly, but lifts the weight. A second test is done using a thinner cable – one with only half the cross-sectional area of the thick cable. This time, the cable stretches, then breaks.

Why did the thinner cable **fail**? Not due to a higher load, as the weight was the same. The **failure** was due to **stress**. Stress is force per unit of area, and is measured in newtons per square metre, or Pascals ($1 \text{ N/m}^2 = 1$ Pa). The thinner cable was therefore **stressed** twice as much as the thick cable, as the same load was **concentrated** into a cross-sectional area that was 50% smaller.

Why did the thick cable stretch but not break? When objects are stressed, they **deform** – that is, they change size (if only slightly). In the tests, the cable **extended** – it increased in length. **Extension** can be measured as a change in an object's length compared with its **original length** before stress was applied. This measurement is called **strain**. According to a law called Young's Modulus of Elasticity, stress is **proportional to** strain. In other words, a percentage increase in stress will cause the same percentage increase in strain. However, this is only true up to a point called the **limit of proportionality**. If a material is **overstressed** – beyond this limit – it will start to become **strained** by a higher proportion. Stress and strain will therefore become **disproportional**.

Small lengths of material, called specimens, can be stressed in a materials testing machine to measure strain and test their strength.

Note: See Unit 18 for more on elasticity and the limit of proportionality.

30.1 Replace the underlined words and expressions with alternative words and expressions from A opposite and Appendix V on page 106.

> If you look at the objects around you, it's difficult to find something that couldn't be smashed with a hammer. But if you laid a hammer down carefully on any of those objects, the (1) <u>force</u> which it (2) <u>put on</u> them wouldn't be sufficient to cause even the slightest damage. This comparison illustrates the difference between:
> * a (3) <u>moving force</u>, which combines mass and movement to apply (4) <u>a shock</u>
> * a (5) <u>still force</u>, which consists only of an object's (6) <u>own mass</u>.
>
> Between the two situations, the (7) <u>size</u> of the load (8) <u>placed on</u> the surface is dramatically different.
>
> The above comparison illustrates another difference in the way surfaces are (9) <u>pressured</u>. When a hammer is laid horizontally on a surface, its weight is spread over a relatively large area. It therefore applies a (10) <u>spread out force</u>. By contrast, when a hammer hits something, only the edge of the hammer head comes into contact with the surface. The force is therefore (11) <u>focused</u> in a small area, applying a (12) <u>localized pressure</u>.

30.2 Complete the technical checklist (1–7) based on the questions (a–g), using words from A and B opposite and Appendix V on page 106. The first one has been done for you.

a Which components need to carry load?
b What types of load will be carried by each part? Which loads will remain constant, and which will differ depending on use and circumstances?
c What amount of load will be exerted, in newtons?
d In what directions will the loads act?
e For the materials used, how concentrated can maximum loads be without putting the component under too much pressure?
f How much deformation can be expected?
g If something breaks, will the assembly collapse dangerously, or in a controlled, relatively safe way?

1 Determine which components are ....load-bearing.......... .
2 Analyze the types of load that will .... on each part. Assess .... loads and .... loads.
3 Calculate the .... of loads as .... quantities.
4 Evaluate loads as .... quantities.
5 Determine the maximum level of .... that can be carried by materials without causing them to be ....
6 Calculate percentages of ....
7 Assess the consequences if a component .... , determining the potential dangers of the ....

Over to you

Think about a machine or structure you're familiar with. Give examples of types of load which act on specific components or members. Say which components are stressed the most, and explain why.

31 Force, deformation and failure

A Types of force and deformation

Non-technical word	Technical term (noun)	Adjective used with the nouns *stress*, *load* and *force*	Initial deformation of component or member
stretching	tension	tensile stress	It will **extend** (lengthen).
squashing	compression	compressive stress	It will **compress** (shorten).
bending	bending	bending stress	It will **bend** – we can also say it will **deflect** or **flex**. Beams usually **sag**, deflecting downwards. In some cases **deflection** or **flexure** is upward – the beam **hogs**.
scissoring	shear or shearing	shear stress	It will deform very little, failing suddenly.
twisting	torsion or torque	torsional stress	It will **twist**.

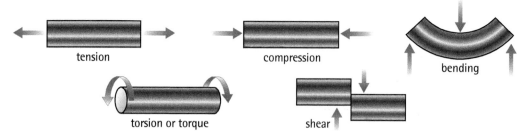

tension   compression   bending

torsion or torque   shear

Bending comprises two opposite stresses: tension and compression. This is shown in the diagram of a **simply supported beam**. As a result of the bending force, the lower half of the beam is **in tension** and the upper half is **in compression**. These opposite stresses reach their maximum at the upper and lower surfaces of the beam, and progressively decrease to zero at the **neutral axis** – an imaginary line along the centre of the beam which is free from stress.

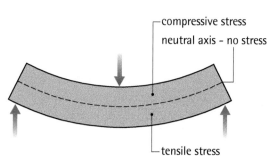

compressive stress
neutral axis - no stress
tensile stress

A simply supported beam

B Types of failure

The ultimate failure of a component or **structural member** depends on the type of force:

- in tension – it will **fracture**
- in compression – if it is thick, it will **crush** (squash). If it is **slender** (long and thin), it will **buckle**, bending out of shape
- **in bending** – it will fracture on the side of the component which is in tension, or crush on the side which is in compression – or fail due to a combination of both
- **in shear** – it will **shear** (break due to shear force)
- **in torsion** – it will fracture or shear.

When vertical members can no longer **resist** a load they either crush or buckle.

31.1 Complete the word puzzle and find the word going down the page. Look at A and B opposite to help you.

1 bend downwards
2 a twisting force
3 take a force without breaking
4 increase in length, due to tension
5 long and thin, likely to buckle rather than crush
6 a scissoring force

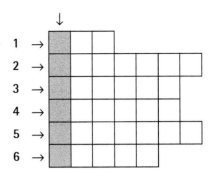

31.2 The question below, which was posted on a forum on a construction website, contains a mistake about a technical fact. Can you find the mistake? Look at A opposite to help you.

Post 1:

I was under the impression that concrete and steel bars were used together in reinforced concrete (RC) because concrete is good at resisting compression and poor at resisting tension, whereas steel is strong in tension. I also thought the steel always went at the bottom of an RC beam because that's the part that's in tension, whereas the top of the beam is free from stress. But if that's the case, when you see reinforcement being fixed in big RC beams, why are there bars both at the bottom and at the top?

31.3 Now complete a structural engineer's answer to the question in 31.2 using the words in the box. Look at A and B opposite and 31.2 above to help you.

bending	compressive	deflect	fracturing	neutral	tensile
compression	crushing	deflection	hog	sag	tension

Replies to post 1:

Let me start by clarifying something. When a beam is subjected to (1) .... stress, the bottom part is generally in tension, as you rightly say. But the top part is not 'free from stress', as you suggest. It's in (2) .... Only the horizontal centreline of the beam – a zone called the (3) .... axis – is not stressed. It's also important to be clear about the strengths of concrete and steel. You're right that concrete is poor at resisting (4) .... stress as it's prone to failure by (5) .... suddenly. It's also true that concrete is good at resisting (6) .... stress. But steel is much stronger than concrete, not just in (7) .... as you point out, but also when it's compressed. So steel is often put in the tops of beams in cases where the beam is subjected to high levels of compression, meaning that the concrete requires reinforcing to prevent it from (8) .... and failing.

Another possible reason for a beam having steel in the top is to take tension. Why would you get tension in the top of a beam? It's true that most beams want to (9) .... downwards because gravity causes them to (10) ...., putting only the bottom of the beam in tension. But in some structures, there are beams or parts of beams that want to (11) .... – being forced into upward (12) ....

Over to you

Think about the different forces acting on a machine or structure you're familiar with. How would the different components or members deform or fail if they were not adequately designed, or if they were overstressed?

32 Structural mechanics

A Statically determinate structures

When a **structural member** – that is, part of a structure – is loaded in a certain direction, the load will cause a **reaction**. This means that another force, equal to the load, will act in the opposite direction. The reaction will **counteract** (resist) the load and stop the **member** from moving. When the loads and reactions acting on a member are equal, we say it is **in equilibrium**. Structures that are designed not to move – to stay in equilibrium – are called **statically determinate structures**.

Note: See Appendix V on page 106 for the names of specific structural members.

B Resultant forces and centre of gravity

Often, a structural member will need to carry different loads of different magnitudes, acting in different directions. To calculate the result of these different **component forces**, an engineer can calculate a **resultant force** (or **resultant**). This is a force with a magnitude and direction equal to all the component forces together.

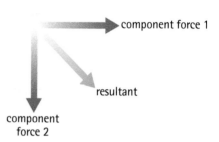

One of the main forces exerted on a structure is gravity. This acts vertically downwards (see Unit 9). Gravity is exerted on every atom of an object. However, to simplify their calculations, engineers assume that gravity is exerted on one imaginary point called the **centre of gravity**. Depending on the shape of the object, this point may be inside the object's cross-sectional area, or outside it (see the diagrams below).

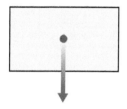
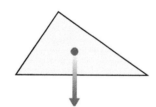

C Frames and trusses

A **frame** (or **framework**) is made from a number of relatively thin members. Examples are bicycle frames and steel-frame buildings. The members of a frame can form a complex shape – often with many triangles – called a **lattice**. The advantage of triangles is that they are **stiff** – they strongly resist deformation. Triangular assemblies can therefore be used to **stiffen** (or **brace**) structures.

1 simple structure

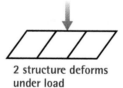
2 structure deforms under load

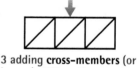
3 adding **cross-members** (or **braces**) stiffens the structure

In diagram 2, the structure deforms because the joints between the thin members are weak and can flex easily. Joints which flex – because they are weak or because they are designed to do so – are called **pin joints**. Lattices which are entirely **pin-jointed**, and which therefore need cross-members to stiffen them, are called **trusses**. A truss contains two types of member. Members that resist tension are called **ties**, and members that resist compression are called **struts**. A joint which does not flex is called a **rigid joint** (or **moment connection**). Rigid joints are often thick and securely joined – for example, by welds.

32.1 Complete the explanation using words and expressions from A opposite. You will need to change the form of one word.

In (1) ...., each load acting on the structure is (2) .... by a (3) .... This means the structure always remains (4) ....

32.2 Complete the text using words and expressions from A, B and C opposite.

> To analyze the roof structure shown in Diagram 1, an engineer draws Diagram 2 to help make some initial, simple calculations. In Diagram 2, the engineer uses the following assumptions and information.
>
> ▸ The three (1) .... forces from the loads act as a single (2) .... force on the top of the frame.
>
> ▸ All the joints in the frame are (3) .... (can flex), so the frame behaves as a (4) ....
>
> ▸ The (5) .... of the roof structure (shown in red) – not including the satellite dish – is exactly halfway between the two supports.

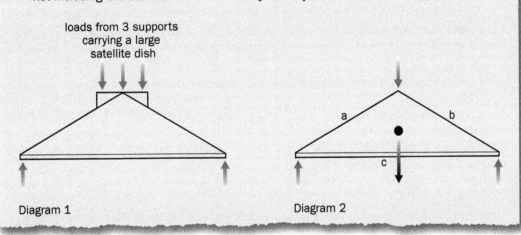

Diagram 1   Diagram 2

32.3 In Diagram 2 above, which of the members (a–c) are ties, and which are struts?

32.4 Choose the correct words from the brackets to complete the sentences. Look at C opposite to help you.

1 Trusses are (frameworks / ties).
2 A connection between members which flexes is called a (pin joint / rigid joint).
3 Struts are designed to resist (compression / tension).
4 By adding cross-members, a frame is (braced / pin-jointed), making it stiffer.

Over to you

Think about a structure or assembly you're familiar with. Answer the following questions:

■ What are the different component forces that act on it?

■ How is it prevented from deforming?

■ How is it affected by gravity?

33 Motion and simple machines

A Acceleration and motion

If an object is **at rest** (not moving) and is free to move (not fixed), an **external force** – a force from outside – will make the object **accelerate**. This means the **velocity** of the object (the speed of its movement in a given direction) will increase. Velocity is measured in **metres per second (m/s)**. If **acceleration** is constant – that is, if the **rate of acceleration** remains the same – it is measured as the increase in velocity (in metres per second) that is achieved each second. The unit of acceleration is therefore metres per second per second – stated as **metres per second squared (m/s^2)**.

If an object is **in motion** (moving) and is subjected to an **opposing force** – that is, one acting on it in the opposite direction – the object will **decelerate**. As with acceleration, **deceleration** is measured in m/s^2. If something moves in a straight line, we say its movement is **linear** – a car accelerating and driving along a straight road is an example of **linear acceleration** and **linear motion**.

On earth, **acceleration due to gravity** is roughly $10 \, m/s^2$. In other words, if an object is dropped and left to **free fall**, its velocity will increase by $10 \, m/s$ every second (not allowing for air resistance). Acceleration and deceleration, such as that generated by aircraft and cars, can be compared with acceleration due to gravity. This relative measure is called **G-force** (G stands for gravity). An acceleration of $10 \, m/s^2$ is measured as **1 G**, $20 \, m/s^2$ as **2 G** (or **2 Gs**), and so on.

B Inertia

The greater the **mass** of an object (see Unit 9), the greater the external force required to cause it to accelerate or decelerate. Resistance to acceleration or deceleration, due to the mass of an object, is called **inertia**. When an object is in motion, its resistance to deceleration, due to inertia, is often called **momentum**.

C Simple machines

The word **machine** generally refers to an assembly which has parts that move. However, a **simple machine** can be a very basic device. A simple machine is something which provides a **mechanical advantage** – that is, the **load** generated by the machine (the force it puts out, or output) is greater than the **effort** (the force put in, or input) required to generate the load.

An example of a simple machine is a **lever**, which is used with a **fulcrum** – a point which acts as a support, and allows the lever to **pivot** (turn around the support). If the lever is placed so that the distance between the effort and the fulcrum is greater than the distance between the load and the fulcrum, a mechanical advantage is created.

In general language, the turning force generated by a lever is called **leverage**. In engineering, a turning force is called a **turning moment** (or **moment**). Moments are calculated by multiplying the distance from the fulcrum, in metres, by the magnitude of the force, in newtons. They are measured in **newton metres (Nm)**.

Note: See Appendix VI on page 108 for more on moments.

BrE: spanner; AmE: wrench

A **spanner** is an example of a lever.

33.1 Complete the article about the *Titanic*, taken from a popular science magazine. Look at A and B opposite to help you.

It's been suggested that the passenger liner *Titanic* wouldn't have sunk after colliding with an iceberg in 1912, if it had hit the obstacle head on and damaged only the front of the ship. As history tells, the crew tried to turn to avoid the iceberg, and 1,517 lives were lost. But how severe would a frontal impact have been for the passengers? The answer depends on several questions:

✽ The ship tried to slow while turning. Would (1) .... deceleration have been more effective, allowing the ship to (2) .... more rapidly?
✽ Based on this (3) .... of deceleration (and assuming the ship would not have stopped in time), what would the (4) .... of the ship have been at the moment of impact?
✽ What was the (5) .... of the iceberg? Calculating the approximate number of kilograms of ice would allow the (6) .... of the iceberg to be compared with the momentum of the *Titanic*. This would show whether the impact would have caused the iceberg to (7) .... to any significant degree, and so absorb some of the shock as it was pushed forward.

Clearly, the above questions depend on numerous unknown variables. So let's make a rough estimate. Let's assume the impact would have occurred at a pretty fast 25 kilometres per hour – that's seven (8) .... And allowing for some shock absorption from bending steel and crushing ice, let's say the ship would have stopped within three seconds (although it would probably have taken longer). This would have resulted in a deceleration of 2.3 (9) .... Expressed as a (10) ...., that gives 0.23 – less than one-third of the deceleration generated by a car braking heavily. So the impact probably wouldn't have caused too much of a shock to the passengers. Whether or not the ship would have sunk, however, is another question.

33.2 Replace the underlined words and expressions with alternative words and expressions from A and B opposite.

The first diagram below illustrates how a worker is able to apply a total (1) <u>force</u> of 50 newtons to the corner of a nut using just his fingers. The distance from the centre of the nut – the point around which the nut (2) <u>turns</u> – and the corner of the nut is 10 mm. This results in a (3) <u>force of leverage</u> of 0.5 newton metres. This is insufficient to tighten the nut properly.

The second diagram shows how a spanner can be used as a (4) <u>tool</u> to provide a (5) <u>boost in force</u>. Applying the same 50-newton force to the end of the 200 mm spanner, which acts as a (6) <u>turning tool</u>, generates 10 newton metres – a force 20 times greater, and enough to tighten the nut.

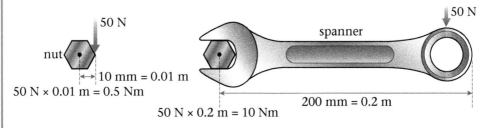

nut
50 N
10 mm = 0.01 m
50 N × 0.01 m = 0.5 Nm
spanner
50 N
200 mm = 0.2 m
50 N × 0.2 m = 10 Nm

Over to you

Think about a simple machine you use or are familiar with. How does it provide a mechanical advantage, and how great is the advantage?

34 Moving parts

A Angular motion

If a spanner is used to tighten a bolt, one end remains in the same position on the bolt, while the other end turns. This type of motion, where one end of a component pivots while the other end follows the arc of a circle, is called **angular motion**. An example is a flap on an aircraft wing, which can be moved to different positions. The point at the centre of angular motion is called the **axis of rotation** (or **axis**). We say that the motion occurs **about the axis** (around it).

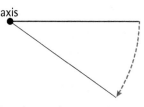
Angular motion

The speed of angular motion is measured as **angular velocity**, and increases in angular velocity are measured as **angular acceleration**.

B Rotary and reciprocating motion

When angular motion is through 360 degrees, it is called a **revolution** (or **rotation**). When moving parts of machines, such as wheels, turn through complete revolutions – once, several times, or for continuous periods – we say they **revolve** (or **rotate**). The **rotational velocity** of **revolving** parts, or **rotating** parts, is measured in **revolutions per minute** (**rpm**) – often called **revs per minute**. The motion of revolving parts is called **rotary motion**.

Rotary motion generates **centrifugal force** – that is, force which pushes outwards, away from the axis of rotation. An increase in rotational velocity results in a higher centrifugal force.

Some components move backwards and forwards. This type of motion is called **reciprocating motion** (or **reciprocating action**) – the component **reciprocates**. In machines, reciprocating motion is often **converted** (changed) to rotary motion. An example is a piston (see Unit 40).

C Engine revs

The abbreviation for revolution – **rev** – is widely used to talk about engines. For example:

A rev counter

- The rotational velocity of an engine is measured by a **rev counter**.
- High and low engine speeds are described as **high revs** and **low revs**.
- Maximum engine speed can be controlled by a **rev limiter**.
- If an engine's **rev limit** is exceeded, we say the engine is **over-revved**.
- An engine designed to run at high speed is a **high-revving** engine.
- When engine speed is increased momentarily, we say the engine is **revved** (or **revved up**).
- We can say an engine is **revved to** a certain speed – for example, revved to 6,000 rpm.

D Friction

Moving parts cause **friction**. Friction is the force of resistance when two surfaces slide against each other. **Frictional resistance** is measured as the **coefficient of friction**. This is the force required to **overcome friction** in order to allow an object made of a specific material to slide along the surface of another specific material.

There are two types of friction. **Static friction** – sometimes called **stiction** – is the frictional resistance between two surfaces that are at rest (not moving). It measures the force needed to start a sliding action. **Dynamic friction** is the friction between two surfaces that are already sliding against each other. It measures the force needed to keep a sliding action going. More force is needed to overcome static friction than to overcome dynamic friction.

34.1 Match the descriptions (1–6) to the terms (a–f). Look at A and B opposite to help you.

1 the speed of movement of a part which turns around a point
2 pressure, exerted in an outward direction, due to rotary motion
3 the rate of increase of speed of a part which turns around a point
4 the point about which a part turns
5 a turning movement
6 movement backwards and forwards

a angular motion
b angular velocity
c angular acceleration
d axis of rotation
e reciprocating motion
f centrifugal force

34.2 Complete the sentences using suitable forms of the words *revolve* or *rotate*. Sometimes forms of both words are possible. Look at B opposite to help you. The first one has been done for you.

1 The measurement of ....*rotational*............ velocity is rpm.
2 As you can see, the wheel .... at extremely high velocity.
3 A recording device counts each .... of the wheel.
4 High-velocity .... motion causes vibration.
5 This wheel is the biggest .... part in the machine.
6 What's the speed of the turbine in .... per minute?
7 The braking system ensures the wheel .... slowly.

34.3 Complete the description of an engine problem using words from C opposite.

Normally, the engine shouldn't be able to run faster than its maximum
(1) .... of 8,000 rpm. The (2) ....
.... should prevent it from exceeding that limit. But
something went wrong, because according to the reading on the
(3) ...., the engine (4) ....
.... 10,500 rpm - so it was (5) ....-..................................
by a significant margin. And since it's not supposed to be a
(6) ....-.................................. engine, it's not designed to cope
with those kinds of speeds.

34.4 Find expressions in D opposite with the following meanings.

1 the measurement of friction
2 the frictional resistance between surfaces that are already sliding against each other
3 the frictional resistance between surfaces that are not yet sliding against each other

Over to you

Describe a machine you know about that contains parts which undergo angular motion and/ or rotary motion.

35 Energy

Forms of energy

The effects of **energy** can be seen, felt or heard in different ways, depending on the **form of energy** in question. The main forms are listed below:

- **kinetic energy**: energy in the form of movement – a type of **mechanical energy**
- **thermal energy**: energy in the form of heat
- **electrical energy**: the energy of an electric current
- **sound energy**: energy in the form of noise
- **light energy**: for example, light emitted from the sun or from a light bulb
- **chemical energy**: energy within substances that can produce a chemical reaction
- **nuclear energy**: energy from an atomic reaction.

Energy cannot be created or destroyed, only **converted** from one form to another. For example, in a torch **powered** by batteries, chemical energy **stored** in the batteries is converted to electrical energy, and the electrical energy is converted to light energy.

Mechanical energy can be stored as **potential energy**. An example is a load, lifted by a crane and suspended at a high level. The weight **has the potential** (in the future) to be released and allowed to fall, becoming kinetic energy. Energy can also be stored when a component is elastically deformed. This is called **strain energy**. An example is the spring in a watch, which is wound up, then progressively unwinds.

Note: For more on deformation, see Unit 18. For more on strain, see Unit 30.

B Energy efficiency

Machines often convert an **energy source**, such as electricity, to another form of **useful energy** – in other words, energy used for a purpose. For example, a motor converts electrical energy (the energy source) into kinetic energy (useful energy). But it also converts some energy into heat and noise. As this will be **dissipated** into the air, and not used, it is **waste energy**.

A motor: electrical energy → useful kinetic energy
→ wasted thermal and sound energy

If a machine converts a high percentage of energy into useful energy, it is **efficient**. For example, if a motor converts 75% of the electrical energy it consumes into kinetic energy, and wastes 25% as thermal and sound energy, it is **seventy-five percent efficient**. Improving **efficiency** – making **efficiency gains** – is a key focus in engineering.

C Work and power

The amount of energy needed to do a task – for example, lifting a load to a certain height by crane – is called **work**. The amount of energy converted in order to perform tasks – in other words, the amount of **work done** – is measured in **joules (J)**. If a force of one newton is required to keep an object moving, the work required to move that object over a distance of one metre is equal to one joule.

The speed, or rate, at which work is done is called **power**, and is measured in **watts (W)**. One watt is one joule per second. Power, in watts, is often referred to as **wattage**. A **powerful** motor will have a higher wattage than a **less powerful** one.

35.1 Make word combinations with *energy* using words from A and B opposite. Then match the combinations with the descriptions (1–8).

1 .... energy = energy stored within the liquids or solids in a battery
2 .... energy = mechanical energy in the form of movement
3 .... energy = potential energy stored in a deformed material
4 .... energy = energy converted to the form required for a purpose
5 .... energy = energy converted to a form that cannot be used
6 .... energy = the form of energy that shines, and can be seen
7 .... energy = the form of energy that can be heard
8 .... energy = energy that results in an increase in temperature

35.2 Complete the article about electric and diesel-electric locomotives using the words in the box. Look at A, B and C opposite to help you.

chemical	efficiency	form	kinetic	powerful	thermal	wattage
convert	efficient	gain	power	source	useful	work
dissipated	electrical	joules	powered	stored	waste	

An electric locomotive is one that is
(1) .... by an external energy
(2) ...., most often via overhead
electric lines. This differs from a diesel-electric
locomotive, which has an onboard fuel tank and
a diesel-powered generator to provide electricity
for its motors. Purely electric power has
numerous advantages over diesel-electric power,
explaining the choice of electric locomotives for
use in high-speed trains.

▲ An electric locomotive

Firstly, an electric locomotive needs to carry neither a generator nor fuel. Its mass is
therefore lower than a diesel-electric equivalent. This results in a significant efficiency
(3) .... , as the electric locomotive's smaller mass means less (4) ....
is done – measured as a total number of (5) .... – on a given journey. For a
comparable rate of acceleration, its motors are also required to provide less
(6) .... As they use a lower (7) ...., this means less (8) ....
motors can be used, making them smaller, thus further reducing weight and improving
(9) .... In addition, electric locomotives use only (10) .... energy.
This means there is no need to (11) .... energy from one (12) .... to
another on board the train (electricity can be generated more efficiently in power stations).

In a diesel-electric unit, the energy conversion process starts with (13) ....
energy, which is (14) .... within the hydro-carbon compounds of diesel. This fuel is
burned to produce (15) .... energy, and the heat is then converted by the engine
into (16) .... energy, which provides the movement to drive the train. This process
is a very long way from being 100% (17) .... – only a small percentage of the
initial chemical energy is converted to the (18) .... energy that is actually used to
drive the train, with a significant percentage being (19) .... into the air in the form
of heat, constituting (20) .... energy.

Over to you

Think about some machines or appliances you're familiar with. What sources of energy do
they convert? What forms of useful energy and waste energy are produced?

36 Heat and temperature

A Changes of temperature and state

The two extracts below are from a basic technical training course for the customer service staff of a manufacturer of heating boilers.

> As you know, **temperature** is measured in **degrees Celsius** (°C). But **heat** is energy, so it's measured in joules. To calculate the amount of energy needed to raise the temperature of a substance, you need to know the mass of the substance being **heated**, and also its **specific heat capacity** – in other words, the amount of energy, in joules, required to raise the temperature of one kilogram of the substance by one degree Celsius.

> What happens when substances change **state**? Well, heat energy is needed to make a solid **melt** and become a liquid. It's also needed to turn liquid into **vapour** – it takes energy to make a liquid **boil**, so that it **evaporates (or vaporizes)** and becomes a gas. That's because **melting** and **evaporation** are **endothermic** processes. That means they take in heat energy – they need to **absorb** heat from a **heat source**, such as a flame. And it's the opposite when a substance **cools**. As a gas **condenses** to become a liquid, or as a liquid **solidifies** to become a solid, the process is **exothermic** – heat is **emitted**. The amount of energy absorbed or emitted while a substance changes state, in joules per kilogram, is called **latent heat**. During melting it's called **latent heat of fusion**, and during vaporizing it's called **latent heat of vaporization**.

Note: See Appendix III on page 100 for other units of temperature, and Appendix VII on page 109 for notes on vapour and **steam**.

B Heat transfer

The textbook extract below looks at **heat transfer** – how heat travels.

To help understand heat transfer, homes provide everyday examples. The **heating systems** in homes often have electric **convector** heaters. These heat the air and make it **circulate**, so that it moves in a circle – first rising, then cooling and sinking before rising again. This is called **convection**, where warm gas or liquid moves around and **dissipates** heat, **transferring** it to the rest of the gas or liquid.

An electric convector heater

Alternatively, the heating system in a home may circulate hot water through **radiators**. The radiators act as **heat exchangers** – devices that transfer heat – in this case, from the hot water inside to the cooler air outside. This happens by **conduction** – heat transfer through solid material. After the heat has been **conducted** through the metal of the radiator, the heat is dissipated by convection.

The third way that heat is transferred is by **radiation**. This is heat that travels as **electromagnetic waves**. An example is the heat from the sun. So the radiators that circulate water have a misleading name, as they don't really function by radiation.

Notes: See Unit 19 for more on the thermal properties of solid materials.
See Appendix VII on page 109 for more on radiators in cooling systems, and **thermal inertia**.
See Appendix VIII on page 110 for specific types of electromagnetic wave.

36.1 Complete the sentences about water using words from A opposite. Sometimes there is more than one possible answer.

1 When the temperature of ice reaches 0 °C, it changes .... – it .... to become water.
2 At 100 °C, water ....
3 When water is .... to 0 °C or below and .... to become ice, it is said to freeze.
4 In gas form, water is called .... or ....
5 Between 100 °C and 374 °C water is a .... because it is below its critical temperature.
6 Extremely hot water vapour is called ....

36.2 Match the two parts to make correct sentences. Look at A and B opposite, and Appendix VII on page 109 to help you.

1 A liquid pumped onto a workpiece that is being machined, to stop it overheating, is called a
2 The form of heat transfer that occurs with infrared heat – a form of electromagnetic wave – is called
3 The metal fins (plates) around air-cooled engines, intended to maximize the surface area of the hot engine that is in contact with the cooler air, are designed to act as a
4 Thick, dense, internal walls inside an energy-efficient house, which are intended to absorb heat energy during the day and store some of it to be emitted at night, function as a
5 The soil and rocks on the surface of the earth remain warm at night in summer, due to the principle of

a radiation.   c heat sink.   e heat exchanger.
b coolant.   d thermal inertia.

36.3 Circle the correct words to complete the article about condensing boilers. Look at A and B opposite to help you. The first one has been done for you.

Condensing boilers are becoming increasingly popular in homes, as they use up to 40% less gas than traditional boilers. How do they work? By exploiting the fact that when a liquid condenses, due to the principle of latent heat of (1) *fusion/vaporization*, the process is (2) *endothermic/exothermic*. This means heat is (3) *absorbed/emitted*, and can thus be (4) *circulated/conducted* via the water inside the radiators in the home.

A condensing boiler burns natural gas (hydrocarbon fuel) to (5) *heat/cool* water, just like a conventional boiler. However, it achieves greater efficiency by recovering energy from water vapour. This is present in the hot, waste gas that's produced when natural gas is burned. In a traditional boiler the (6) *heat/temperature* energy from the gas, which is at a (7) *heat/temperature* of 180 °C or more, would be (8) *dissipated/radiated* into the atmosphere by (9) *conduction/convection*, and the water vapour within it would condense in the outside air. But in a condensing boiler the hot gas passes through a (10) *heat/temperature* exchanger. This allows the heat from the gas to be (11) *absorbed/emitted* by the cool water that's returning to the boiler after passing through the radiators in the home's (12) *cooling/heating* system – heat transfer takes place from hot gas to cool water by (13) *conduction/radiation* through the metal of the heat exchanger. In addition, when the temperature of the gas has fallen to a certain point, the water vapour within it (14) *condenses/solidifies*. And it is this process that enables significant amounts of heat to be transferred, due to the principle of (15) *latent/specific* heat.

Over to you

Think about some appliances, machines or structures where heat transfer is an important consideration. How is the heat transferred, and how does this affect the design?

37 Fluid containment

A Pipes, ducts and hoses

A pipe

An air duct

A hose

Pipes are rigid tubes, made from materials such as steel and plastic. They carry **fluids** (liquids or gases). Pipes can be fitted together with different **pipe fittings** (see Appendix IX on page 111). Assemblies of pipes are often referred to as **pipework**.

Mains are underground pipes for water and natural gas. **Water mains** and **gas mains** run beneath the streets of cities to supply buildings.

Pipelines are long-distance pipes, often above ground, for crude oil or natural gas.

Drains are underground pipes that carry waste water. Large drains, as found below the streets in cities, are called **sewers**. Drains and sewers rely on gravity to allow them to flow. They therefore have a downward slope, called a **fall**.

Ducts are pipes used for moving air that is not under pressure – usually for heating or air-conditioning. **Ductwork** often consists of rectangular cross-section ducts.

Hoses are flexible tubes, often made from plastic, for liquids and gases. They are fitted together using **hose fittings** (or **hose couplings**). Examples of hoses are fuel hoses and compressed air hoses – sometimes called **fuel lines** and **air lines**.

Note: In everyday English, **fluid** usually means a liquid. In physics and engineering, the word refers to both liquids and gases.

B Tanks

A **tank** is a container for liquid or gas. It may be **watertight** (will not leak water) and open at the top. It may also be enclosed and **airtight** (will not leak gas), and may contain gas that is under pressure.

A **pressure vessel** is a tank for storing gas – or a mixture of liquid and gas – that is under pressure. The **vessel** must therefore be **sealed** – with no openings, so that gas cannot escape. It must also be strong enough to withstand the pressure inside. Pressure vessels include small portable **gas cylinders** (also called **gas bottles**). Some pressure vessels also function as **boilers** – they heat the liquid inside them in order to boil it and increase pressure – for example, a water boiler that produces high-pressure steam.

C Pumps, fans and turbines

Liquids can be forced to **flow** (move) along pipes by mechanical devices called **pumps**. For example, in cars, fuel is **pumped** from the fuel tank to the engine by a fuel pump. The **flow** of fluids can be controlled by **valves** (see Appendix IX on page 111). A pump used to increase the pressure of gas is called a **compressor**.

A device powered by a motor which rotates in order to move air or gas – for example, along a duct – is called a **fan**. A **turbine** has the opposite function to a fan – it is designed to be moved by a flow of air or gas. For example, a **wind turbine** revolves due to the wind, and can be used to drive a generator (to generate electricity).

This compressor produces **compressed air** for powering tools.

37.1 Complete the emails about the design of a new manufacturing plant using words from A opposite.

New Message

Air temperature will be high in this area, due to the presence of four large-diameter steel steam (1) .... running along the ceiling. This opens up the possibility of extracting hot air and transferring it, via (2) ...., to other areas of the plant, for heating use.

New Message

Given that this machine will move to an extent, due to vibration, it should be connected to the water supply using a flexible (3) ...., rather than a rigid (4) ....
The pressure of the supply may also need to be increased, depending on the pressure of water coming into the plant from the (5) ....

New Message

Waste water will exit the plant via a (6) .... on the western edge of the site. This will run into the (7) .... under the street on the north side of the plant. The survey has confirmed that the level of the site, relative to the street, will allow an adequate (8) ....

37.2 One sentence in each pair is false. Choose the true sentence. Look at A and B opposite and Appendix IX on page 111 to help you.

1 a All gas cylinders are pressure vessels.
  b All pressure vessels are gas cylinders.
2 a Elbows are types of pipe or hose fitting.
  b Pipe or hose fittings are types of elbow.
3 a Any watertight tank will also be airtight.
  b Any airtight tank will also be watertight.
4 a All pressure vessels are types of tank.
  b All tanks are types of pressure vessel.
5 a A pipe is a specific sort of pipeline.
  b A pipeline is a specific sort of pipe.

A propane gas tank

37.3 Change one word in each of the sentences below to make them correct. Look at C opposite and Appendix IX on page 111 to help you.

1 A fan is designed to be driven by a flow of air or gas.
2 A pump used to increase the pressure in a vessel is called a turbine.
3 A safety valve is an inlet which releases excess pressure.
4 A non-return valve is also called a safety valve.
5 Some valves can be partly closed to stop a flow, reducing its rate.

Over to you

Think about a machine or installation you're familiar with, in which liquid or gas is stored, supplied or circulated. What equipment is used to contain the gas or liquid? How are flow and pressure managed?

38 Fluid pressure

A Gauge pressure and absolute pressure

Pressure is the amount of force acting on an area. When **fluids** (liquids or gases) are **under pressure** they **exert pressure on** the surfaces of the tanks, pipes, etc., that hold them. Examples of **pressurized** fluids are **compressed air** inside air hoses, **compressed gases** such as propane in gas cylinders, and water in water mains. The SI measurement of pressure is the **Pascal**. One Pascal is equal to one newton per square metre ($1 \text{ Pa} = 1 \text{ N/m}^2$). However, many **pressure gauges** (devices which measure pressure) use the imperial measurement **pounds per square inch** (**psi**). Pressure can also be measured in **bars**. One bar is roughly equal to **atmospheric pressure** – that is, the pressure of the air in the atmosphere – at sea level. For example, **four bars**, or **four bar** – which can also be described as **four atmospheres** – is four times atmospheric pressure.

When engineers calculate the pressure of a fluid inside a vessel, they usually calculate its **gauge pressure**. This is the **pressure differential** – the difference in pressure – between the fluid inside the vessel and atmospheric pressure outside. Therefore, with gauge pressure, it is assumed that the atmosphere has a pressure of zero Pascals – even though this is not true (see below). Engineers use gauge pressure because they need to know if a fluid inside a vessel is **at a higher pressure** or **at a lower pressure** than **the outside air** (the air in the atmosphere), and if it is, by how much. This allows them to design tanks and pipes so that they do not fail dangerously by **exploding** if their gauge pressure is positive, or by **imploding** if their gauge pressure is negative.

Pressure can also be measured by comparing it with a **vacuum** – a void containing no gas or liquid, as in space, where pressure is truly zero Pascals. Pressure compared with a vacuum is called **absolute pressure**. The absolute pressure of the atmosphere at sea level is approximately 100,000 Pascals (or 100 kilo-Pascals). Therefore a **partial vacuum** – which is below atmospheric pressure but is not a **perfect vacuum** – has a **positive pressure** when it is measured as an absolute pressure, because it has a higher pressure than a perfect vacuum. But it has a **negative pressure** when it is measured as a gauge pressure, because it has a lower pressure than the atmosphere.

Note: See Appendix III on page 100 for more on imperial measurements.

B Hydrostatic pressure and siphonic action

In liquids – most often in water – pressure and flow can be generated by **hydrostatic pressure**. An example is a water tower which supplies drinking water to homes. Water is stored in the tower at a high level, so that the water pushes down. This is called a **head of water**. It puts the water at lower level (in the water main) under pressure. If the height of the water tower is increased, this will increase the water pressure at low level. Smaller tanks located at a high level to generate hydrostatic pressure – at the tops of buildings, for example – are called **header tanks**.

Note: See Appendix X on page 112 for a description of **siphonic action**.

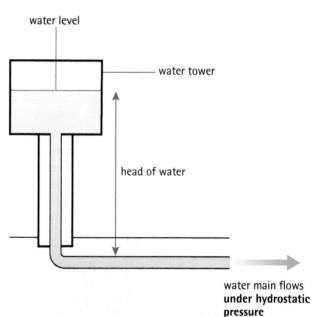

water level

water tower

head of water

water main flows **under hydrostatic pressure**

38.1 Complete the sentences using the words *positive*, *negative* and *zero*.

1 In a perfect vacuum, absolute pressure is .... and gauge pressure is ....
2 In a partial vacuum, absolute pressure is .... and gauge pressure is ....
3 At atmospheric pressure, absolute pressure is .... and gauge pressure is
....
4 In compressed air, absolute pressure is .... and gauge pressure is ....

38.2 Use the expressions in the box to complete the article about pressurized aircraft cabins, taken from an engineering journal. Look at A opposite to help you.

at a higher pressure	compressed air	gauge pressure	pressurized
at a lower pressure	exert pressure on	one atmosphere	outside air
atmospheric pressure	explode	pressure differential	

Ever wondered about ... **pressurized aircraft cabins?**

It's a well-known fact that the cabins of commercial aircraft are (1) .... This is an obvious requirement, given that at high altitude the air is (2) .... than (3) .... at ground level. If passengers were exposed to these conditions while flying at altitude, they would suffer numerous health problems. Hence the need, at high altitude, to maintain the air inside the fuselage (4) .... than the (5) .... But how is this achieved and controlled?

At the moment an aircraft's doors are closed at the airport, the cabin pressure is clearly equivalent to (6) ...., meaning the (7) .... of the cabin is zero. Once the aircraft takes off and begins to climb, the pressure of the outside air will begin to decrease, while air pressure inside the aircraft remains the same thanks to the airtight fuselage.

However, maintaining the air pressure simply by keeping the same air inside the aircraft for the duration of a flight would be problematic – firstly because the air needs to be continually renewed for the comfort of passengers, and secondly because at very high altitude the significant (8) .... between the inside and outside of the cabin would (9) .... the inside of the fuselage to an unacceptably high degree. Although the resulting stresses would not be high enough to cause the fuselage to (10) ...., they would result in a high rate of metal fatigue. Consequently, as the aircraft climbs, air is released through valves in the fuselage until a slightly lower pressure is attained – equivalent to the pressure of the outside air at an altitude of between 5,000 and 8,000 feet. Air is then constantly renewed during the flight by releasing it through the valves, and replacing the equivalent volume with (11) .... pressurized to the same level by the aircraft's engines.

38.3 Match the two parts to make correct sentences. Look at B opposite and Appendix X on page 112 to help you.

1 Header tanks are designed to
2 To *prime* means to
3 Siphonic action is able to
4 Water towers are large tanks designed to

a make liquid flow upwards from its surface.
b generate hydrostatic pressure in a building.
c supply large numbers of buildings.
d fill a pipe or hose to its full bore, removing the air.

Over to you

Think about a system you're familiar with which contains fluid that is at a higher or lower pressure than atmospheric pressure. What is the reason for having a positive or negative pressure? How great is the pressure differential, relative to atmospheric pressure? How is the pressure differential generated and maintained?

39 Fluid dynamics

A Fluid dynamics and aerodynamics

Fluid dynamics is the study of how gases and liquids flow around objects. The branch of fluid dynamics concerned with **airflow** – called **aerodynamics** – is relevant to the design of aircraft, vehicles and structures. Aerodynamic tests can be done in **wind tunnels** – tunnels through which air is blown at high velocity. Analysis can also be done using **computational fluid dynamics (CFD)** – computers with complex simulation software.

B Drag

Aerodynamic drag (or **drag**) is the resistance of an object to an airflow. It is measured by the **drag coefficient**. Objects with a low drag coefficient have little force exerted on them by an airflow. We say they are **streamlined**. There are different types of drag:

- **Form drag** is due to the shape of the object.
- **Skin friction** is the drag caused by air flowing over the surface of the object.
- **Pressure drag** is the pressure differential between the air **upstream of** the object (flowing towards it) and the air **downstream of** it (flowing away behind it). The lower-pressure zone close behind a moving object is often called the **slipstream**.
- **Interference drag** depends on the amount of **turbulence** around the object.

C Laminar flow and turbulent flow

In aerodynamics, engineers focus on the airflow in the **boundary layer** – the air close to the surface of an object. If the object is streamlined, the airflow in the boundary layer will be **laminar**, following a direct, clean path. With a less streamlined object, the airflow will be **turbulent**, flowing in a disturbed, messy fashion. A **turbulent flow** produces more drag than a **laminar flow**, and generates a bigger **wake** – that is, the V-shaped zone of turbulent air behind the object. Wakes contain **vortices**. A **vortex** is a twisting flow – like water going down the plughole in a bath.

D Aerofoils

Aerofoils are components designed to make air flow in specific ways. They include:

- aircraft **wings,** which generate **lift** – that is, upward aerodynamic force
- the **blades** of plane **propellers**, and helicopter **rotor blades**, which generate **thrust** to **propel** aircraft through the air
- wings on racing cars, which generate **downforce** – downward aerodynamic force.

An aircraft propeller with two blades

Aerofoils have specially designed **profiles** (cross-sectional shapes), often with their **leading edge** – the front edge, relative to the airflow – shaped differently to their **trailing edge**, at the rear. The behaviour of air around an aerofoil depends on the velocity of the airflow, and also on the **angle of attack** (or **pitch**) of the aerofoil – its angle relative to the airflow.

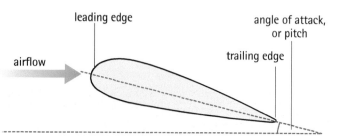

leading edge

angle of attack, or pitch

trailing edge

airflow

BrE: aerofoil; AmE: airfoil

The section of an aircraft wing – an example of an aerofoil

39.1 Sort the terms in the box into categories (1–5). Look at A, B, C and D opposite to help you.

| CFD | form drag | rotor | slipstream | wind tunnel |
| downforce | lift | skin friction | wake | wing |

1 Types of aerodynamic resistance: .... and ....
2 Aerodynamic forces acting in specific directions: .... and
....
3 Aerodynamic effects downstream of an object: .... and ....
4 Types of aerofoil: a .... and a ....
5 Aerodynamic analysis tools: .... and a ....

39.2 Use one term from each category in 39.1 to complete the sentences below. Look at A, B and C opposite to help you.

1 The widening zone of turbulent air behind a fast-moving vehicle is called the
....
2 In very strong winds, the low pressure generated just above the sheltered sides of the roofs of buildings generates ...., which can cause the roof to 'explode' outwards due to the higher-pressure air inside the building.
3 The aerodynamic effectiveness of designs can be tested in a ....
4 On an aircraft fuselage, the heads of rivets are designed to be as flat as possible in order to limit ....
5 Most helicopters have either two or three main ....

39.3 Use the words in the box to complete the article, taken from a popular science magazine. You will need to use some words twice. Look at B, C and D opposite to help you.

| aerofoil | angle | boundary | drag | laminar | leading | trailing |
| airflow | attack | downforce | flow | layer | pitch | turbulent |

In aerodynamic-speak, the term 'spoiler' is slightly confusing, as it has two different meanings. In automotive engineering, a spoiler is a wing-like (1) .... on the back of a car. Unlike the wings on racing cars, the purpose of spoilers on road cars is not to generate (2) ...., but to 'spoil' or disrupt the (3) .... within the (4) ....
.... – the air close to the surface of the car's body. While this may seem strange, by turning what would otherwise be a smooth, (5) .... into a messy, (6) ....
..............................., the car's (7) .... coefficient can be reduced, and the vehicle's handling can be made more stable at higher speeds.

In aeronautical engineering, spoilers – also called airbrakes – are aerofoils mounted on the tops of an aircraft's wings. When deployed – most often at the moment a plane lands – they rotate in an angular motion, with their (8) .... edge (near the front of the wing) acting as a pivot, while the (9) .... edge (at the rear) lifts, increasing the spoiler's (10) .... Spoilers serve a dual purpose. Firstly, they generate (11) ...., helping to push the aircraft down onto the runway. Secondly, they create (12) ...., increasing air resistance and helping to slow the aircraft down.

Spoilers are therefore different to flaps, which are deployed from the rear of an aircraft's wings as it descends and slows down before landing. Flaps are rotated downwards, at a progressively increasing (13) .... of ...., in order to provide increased lift at lower speeds.

Over to you

Describe how a specific aircraft, vehicle or structure is affected by airflow. How does air flow around it? Which aerodynamic issues do you think engineers needed to consider in its design?

40 Engines and motors

A Types and functions of engines and motors

The term **engine** usually refers to **petrol engines**, **diesel engines** and **jet engines** (or **jets**). In engineering, **motor** usually means **electric motor** – but in general language, 'motor' can also refer to petrol and diesel engines. Engines and motors **power** (or **drive**) machines by generating rotary motion – for example, to drive wheels. In jet engines, compressors and turbines rotate to generate **thrust** – pushing force, produced by forcing air from the back of the engine at high velocity.

A jet engine

As an engine produces a **couple** – rotary force – the moving parts of the machine it is driving will produce resistance, due to friction and other forces. As a result, **torque** (twisting force) is exerted on the output shaft of the engine. Torque – calculated as a turning moment, in newton metres – is therefore a measure of how much rotational force an engine can exert. The rate at which an engine can work to exert torque is the **power** of the engine, measured in **watts**. Although engineers normally calculate engine power in watts, the power of vehicle engines is often given in **brake horsepower** (**bhp**). This is the power of an engine's output shaft measured in **horsepower** (**hp**) – a historic measurement of power (see Appendix III on page 100).

Note: See the following units for more information: Unit 33 (turning moments), Unit 34 (rotary motion), Unit 35 (power), and Unit 41 (shafts).

> BrE: petrol; AmE: gasoline
> BrE: petrol engine; AmE: gasoline engine

B Internal combustion engines

Petrol and diesel engines are **internal combustion engines**. This means they are driven by the **combustion** (burning) of fuel in enclosed, sealed spaces called **combustion chambers**. In petrol and diesel engines, the combustion chambers are **cylinders** surrounded by a **cylinder block** and closed at the top by a **cylinder head**. Each cylinder contains a **piston**. The number of **piston cylinders** in an engine varies – engines in small motorcycles have only one, while sports car engines may have twelve.

Fuel is supplied to each cylinder from a tank. In most engines, the flow of fuel is generated by a pump, which forces it – at high pressure – through **fuel injectors**. These vaporize the fuel, allowing it to mix with air. Using this **mixture** (of fuel and air), most engines function as **four-stroke engines**. This means they work on a **cycle** of four stages – or four **strokes**. A stroke is an upward or downward movement of a piston.

1 Induction or intake	2 Compression	3 Power or ignition	4 Exhaust
The **intake valve** opens. The mixture enters the cylinder through a **port** (opening) in the cylinder head while the piston moves downwards.	The intake valve closes. The piston moves upwards, compressing the mixture.	The **spark plug** produces a spark, which **ignites** (lights) the mixture. On ignition, the mixture explodes, generating a sudden pressure which forces the piston down.	The **exhaust valve** opens, and the piston moves upwards, forcing the **exhaust gases** – those produced during combustion – out of the cylinder via the exhaust port. The exhaust valve then closes and the cycle begins again.

The cycle of a four-stroke petrol engine

Notes: See exercise 40.2 opposite for an illustration of a cylinder.
See Unit 42 for more on **cam**, **camshaft**, **connecting rod** and **crankshaft**.

40.1 Complete the text about diesel engines using words from A and B opposite.

Diesel engines differ from (1) .... engines in one key respect: they are not fitted with a (2) .... , in each cylinder, to ignite the fuel. This is because when a (3) .... of diesel and air is compressed inside a hot (4) .... , it will explode spontaneously, without the need for a spark to provide (5) .... A diesel engine must therefore work in a way which prevents the diesel from exploding before the piston is at the top of the cylinder. To achieve this, the engine takes in only air during the (6) .... stage of the cycle. Therefore, during the (7) .... stage, only air – and not an air–fuel mixture – is pressurized. It is only at that last instant, when full compression has occurred, that the (8) .... above each cylinder forces vaporized diesel into the combustion chamber, where it ignites.

Diesel engines operate at lower speeds than petrol engines, making them less suitable for high-speed applications. However, they are more able to (9) .... heavy vehicles, as they can produce greater amounts of (10) .... than petrol engines.

40.2 Look at the cross-section of an engine, and label it using words and expressions from B opposite.

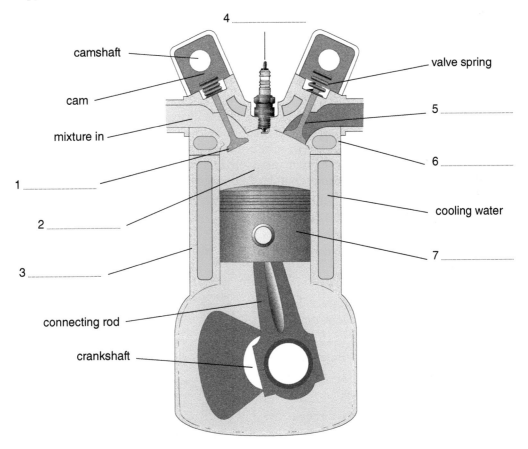

One cylinder of a four-stroke internal combustion engine

Over to you

Think about the engine in a vehicle you're familiar with. Describe specific aspects of it – the type of fuel it uses, the number of cylinders it has, and how much power and torque it produces.

41 Transmission 1

A Gears

Gear wheels, or **gears**, are wheels with **teeth** (or **cogs**). The teeth **interlock** (fit together) with those of other gear wheels. When one gear wheel revolves, the other revolves with it – in the opposite direction – as their teeth **mesh together**. Gears are normally fitted to **shafts**. They **transmit** rotary motion from one shaft to another – that is, they transmit **drive**. Drive, usually supplied by an engine or motor, causes a shaft to revolve. A shaft connected directly to an engine or motor is called a **driveshaft** – or an **input shaft**. A gear wheel on a driveshaft is called a **driver**. The second gear wheel, which **meshes with** the driver, is called a **follower** – the driver **drives** the follower.

An assembly of several shafts and gear wheels is called a **gear train** or **transmission system**. It begins with an input shaft and ends with an **output shaft**. The system may contain **idler gears** (or **idlers**). These change the direction of a follower.

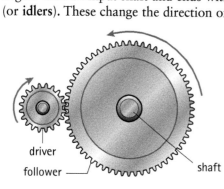

driver
follower —
shaft

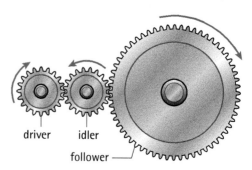

driver   idler
follower —

B Gear ratios

Gears can provide a mechanical advantage (see Unit 33) by using different **gear ratios**. In the diagrams above, the driver has 20 teeth and the follower has 60 teeth. Therefore the driver rotates three times to make the follower rotate once. So the gear ratio is **3:1** (**three to one**). This means that if, for example, the **input speed** – that is, the speed of the driver – is 3,000 rpm, the **output speed** (of the follower) will be 1,000 rpm.

In some machines, a **gearbox** is used to provide a number of different gear ratios. A gearbox has a **gear selection** system, which allows gears to be **changed** (or **shifted**) while the transmission is running. This may be a **manual gearbox**, where gears are changed by a person, or an **automatic gearbox**, which automatically **selects** a **higher gear** or **lower gear**, as needed.

C Types of gear wheel

- **Spur gears** are the simplest gears. The teeth run straight across the wheel.

- **Helical gears** have curved teeth, so that they mesh together more smoothly.

- **Bevel gears** allow drive to be transmitted through an angle – often 90°.

- **Crown gears** transmit drive through 90°, often to a small gear called a **pinion**.

- **Worm gears** transmit drive through an angle. They also allow a low output speed relative to the input speed of the **worm**. They can provide a 'one way' drive, as a worm can drive a gear but a gear cannot drive a worm (the mechanism will lock).

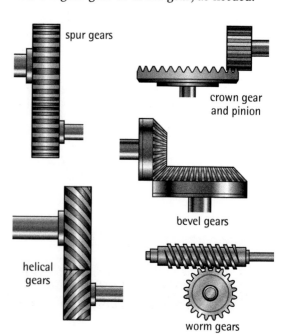

spur gears

crown gear
and pinion

bevel gears

helical
gears

worm gears

41.1 Change four words in the text below to make it correct. Look at A opposite to help you.

> An engine is connected to a driveshaft. Fitted to this output shaft is a gear wheel called the idler. As this gear wheel turns, it drives another gear wheel alongside it called a driver, which is fitted to an input shaft.

41.2 Complete the text about continuously variable transmission using the words in the box. Look at A, B and C opposite to help you.

automatic	higher	ratio	shafts	transmit
helical	manual	selection	shift	wheels

CONTINUOUSLY VARIABLE TRANSMISSION (CVT)

(1) .... gearboxes allow the driver of a vehicle to (2) .... gears as required. If a (3) .... gear is selected, the speed of the output shaft will increase relative to the input shaft, for a given engine speed. In a typical (4) .... gearbox, however, the gear (5) .... system is automated, requiring no action by the driver. In addition, most automatic transmission systems use so-called planetary gears. In basic terms, these allow the transmission to remain connected at all times – unlike manual gearboxes, in which pairs of (6) .... gears are momentarily disconnected each time a shift is made.

The principle of continually variable transmission (CVT) is entirely different to both manual and automatic systems. Instead of having a fixed number of different gear (7) .... , each with different numbers of teeth, CVT uses a special mechanism to continuously and progressively adjust the gear (8) .... between the input and output (9) .... Therefore, as the vehicle accelerates or decelerates, continual adjustments are made to the transmission automatically. This allows the engine to be maintained at a constant speed for optimum power and fuel efficiency while the system is able to continuously (10) .... drive to the vehicle's wheels.

The Case-IH Puma CVX tractor is equipped with continuously variable transmission.

41.3 Make word combinations with *gears* using words from A and C opposite. Then use the word combinations to complete the sentences (1–4) below. Sometimes there is more than one possible answer.

1 .... gears are used to transmit drive through an angle.
2 .... gears run more quietly than spur gears.
3 .... gears can generally only transmit drive in one direction.
4 .... gears allow drivers and followers to revolve in the same direction.

Over to you

Think about the transmission system in a machine or vehicle you're familiar with. Describe how drive is transmitted from the input shaft to the output shaft.

42 Transmission 2

A Chains, sprockets and pulleys

Drive can be transmitted from one shaft to another, across a distance, by **roller chains** (or **chains**). Chains drive, or are driven by, toothed wheels called **sprockets**. Pairs of sprockets with different numbers of teeth can provide different gear ratios. A bicycle is an example of a machine with **chain drive**.

Belt drive works in a similar way to chain drive. **Belts** are usually smooth and are fitted around smooth **pulley wheels** (or **sheaves**). However, **toothed belts** and toothed pulley wheels can be used in applications where a smooth belt could slip. A combination of several **pulleys** can give a mechanical advantage – for example, in cranes to lift heavy loads. In this case, **cables** – also called **wire ropes** – are used instead of belts.

Notes: **Pulley** may refer to pulley wheels and belts together, or to a pulley wheel only.
    See Unit 33 for more on mechanical advantage.

B Conversion between reciprocating and rotary motion

The reciprocating linear motion of pistons is converted to rotary motion by **connecting rods** (or **conrods**) and a **crankshaft**. The shape of the crankshaft allows the connecting rods to exert force at a distance from its centre. This increases the turning moment they generate. Bicycle pedals are an example of a simple **crank**.

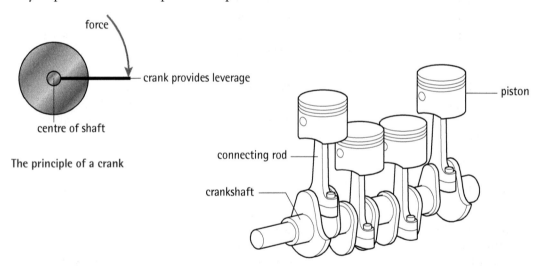

The principle of a crank

In an engine, a heavy wheel – called a **flywheel** – is fitted to the end of the crankshaft. This provides momentum, giving the pistons more constant motion.

As well as driving a machine or vehicle, the motion of an engine's crankshaft is used to open and close the valves in the cylinder head. Rotary motion is transmitted, often via a toothed belt or chain, to the **camshaft** at the top of the engine. The **cams** fixed on the camshaft cause **followers** – which are connected to the valves – to move up and down as the cam revolves. As they move, they open and close the valves.

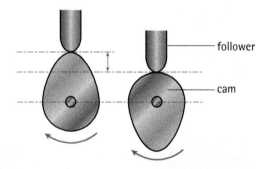

Notes: See the following units for more information: Unit 33 (momentum and turning moments), Unit 34 (rotary and reciprocating motion), and Unit 40 (internal combustion engines). See Appendix XI on page 113 for more on mechanisms used with rotary motion.

42.1 Circle the correct words to complete the text about how chain drive works on bicycles. Look at A opposite and Appendix XI on page 113 to help you.

> On a bicycle, the pedals – which provide support for the rider's feet – are fitted to a (1) *crank / sheave* at either side of the frame. These are fixed together by a short shaft, called a spindle, which runs through a tube at the bottom of the frame. The tube contains (2) *bearings / roller chains*, which allow the spindle to turn freely. A (3) *pulley / sprocket*, fitted to the shaft, drives a (4) *cable / chain*, which drives a second (5) *crank / sprocket* at the rear of the bike. This turns the rear wheel.

42.2 Complete the text about the advantages of chain drive on bicycles, using the words in the box. You will need to use some words more than once. Look at A opposite to help you.

belt	chain	pulley	sprocket	toothed	wheel

> The advantages of using chain drive on bicycles are:
> - its ability to transmit drive over a distance – from the centre of the bike to the rear
> - that a (1) .... will not slip as it travels around a (2) .... – unlike a (3) ...., which is more likely to slip as it travels around a (4) ....
> ....
> - that the teeth on a (5) .... will force dirt out of the holes in a (6) .... , whereas dirt would become trapped between a (7) .... and a (8) .... – a problem which would make a (9) .... belt unsuitable for overcoming the problem of slipping.

42.3 Answer the questions below using words from B opposite and Appendix XI on page 113.

1 In an engine, which revolving component generates the up-and-down motion required to open and close a valve in the cylinder head?
2 How can the motion of an engine's crankshaft be transmitted to the camshaft?
3 What term is given to a component which presses against a cam and moves with a reciprocating action?
4 Which component is heavy and helps an engine to run smoothly?
5 Which two engine components are joined by a connecting rod?
6 What component could be used to connect the end of a crankshaft to a driveshaft that is at 20 degrees to the crankshaft?
7 In vehicles, what friction mechanism (controlled by the driver) is used to gradually transmit drive to the wheels, via the gearbox?
8 In disc brakes, what term is given to the components that are pressed against the brake disc to generate friction?

Over to you

Think about a machine you're familiar with which uses chain or belt drive, or one which converts reciprocating motion to rotary motion (or vice versa). Describe the mechanisms used, and explain their functions.

43 Current, voltage and resistance

A Electric current

The photo on the opposite page shows a simple **electric circuit** (or **circuit**). A **cell** provides an **electric current** (or **current**). This flows through wires, which **conduct** the electricity (provide a way for it to travel). The current is used to light a **lamp**. So, like all circuits, the example includes:

- an **electrical supply** – in this case, the cell
- an **electrical conductor** (or **conductor**) – an electrical path – in this case, wires
- one or more **electrical components** (or **components**) – electrical devices (in this case, the lamp) which have a function.

Current – measured in **amperes**, or **amps** (**A**) – is the rate of flow of **electric charge**. Electric charge is carried by **electrons** – particles with a **negative charge** (–), which are normally attached to atoms. When an electric current **flows** through a conductor, the electrons move from one atom to another – in the case of a copper wire, from one copper atom to the next. If the number of electrons flowing through a conductor increases, then the **amperage**, or **ampage** (current) increases. When electrons flow, carrying a current, they can be called **charge carriers**.

Notes: In everyday English, **cells** are called **batteries**. In technical English, a **battery** is a number of cells placed together.
Lamps are often called **bulbs** in everyday English.

B Voltage and resistance

The amount of current (in amps) flowing through a circuit will partly depend on the **electromotive force** (**EMF**) of the electrical supply. Electromotive force is measured in **volts** (**V**), and is generally called **voltage**. The voltage depends on the 'strength' of the electrical supply. In the diagram above, adding a second cell would supply a higher voltage.

The amount of current will also depend on **electrical resistance** (or **resistance**). This value – in **ohms** (Ω) – is a measure of how easily current can flow through the conductors and components in a circuit. For example, a lamp creates resistance because the **filament** – the metal wire inside it – is very thin. This limits the amount of current that can flow. Resistance also depends on the materials used as conductors. For example, copper has a low resistance and so is a good conductor.

Materials with very high resistance, such as plastics, are called **electrical insulators** (or **insulators**). Only very high voltages cause current to flow through them. Materials that are good insulators are used to **insulate** conductors. An example is plastic **insulation** around electric wires. This stops people from touching the conductor and – if it is **live** (carrying current) – from getting a dangerous **electric shock**.

C Electrical power

The text below, about **electrical power**, is from a home improvements magazine.

The amount of current, in amps, required by an **electrical appliance** – such as a TV or an electric kettle – depends on the **power** of the appliance. This number – expressed in **watts** (**W**) – will be marked somewhere on the appliance. To calculate the required current, simply take the **wattage** and divide it by the voltage of the electrical supply in your home – around 230 volts in most of Europe. Therefore, for an electric kettle with a **power rating** of 2,000 watts (as specified by the manufacturer), the current required is:

$$\frac{2{,}000 \text{ watts}}{230 \text{ volts}} = 8.7 \text{ amps}$$

43.1 Complete the word puzzle and find the word going down the page. Look at A, B and C opposite page to help you.

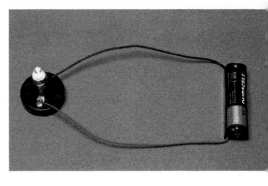

1 another term for amperage
2 provided by a battery, for example
3 measured as a wattage
4 allows current to flow through it
5 has very high electrical resistance
6 carried by moving electrons
7 another term for an electrical 'device'
8 the consequence of a person touching a live conductor

1	ELECTRIC	
2	ELECTRIC	
3	ELECTRIC	
4	ELECTRIC	
5	ELECTRIC	
6	ELECTRIC	
7	ELECTRIC	
8	ELECTRIC	

43.2 Complete the extract about current and power calculations using the words in the box. Look at A, B and C opposite to help you.

amps	conductor	current	resistance	voltage	wattage
components	circuit	ohms	supply	volts	watts

In electrical calculations, electromotive force is expressed by the letter E, resistance by the letter R, and current by the letter I (which comes from the word 'intensity').

According to Ohm's Law: I = E/R.

In other words, the (1) .... flowing through a (2) ...., measured in (3) ...., equals the (4) .... of the electrical (5) ...., measured in (6) ...., divided by the total (7) ...., measured in (8) .... To work out the value of R, it is necessary to calculate the total resistance of all the (9) .... and connecting lengths of (10) .... that make up the circuit.

Once both the voltage and amperage are known, it is possible to work out the power, measured in (11) ...., that will be consumed. Power (P) can be calculated using the equation P = EI. Therefore (12) .... equals voltage multiplied by amperage.

Over to you

Say how much power is required by an electrical appliance you know about, and what voltage and current are used to power it. Then use these values to calculate and state what the total resistance of the appliance is.

44 Electrical supply

A Direct current and alternating current

The current from a cell is **direct current (DC)** – a constant flow of electricity which travels around a circuit in one direction. The electricity supplied to homes and other buildings – called **mains electricity** – is **alternating current (AC)**. Unlike a **DC supply**, an **AC supply** flows backwards and forwards – its direction continually **alternates**. The rate at which the current alternates – called the **frequency** – is measured in **hertz (Hz)**. For example, in the UK, AC supply is 50 Hz – it alternates 50 times per second. On a graph, the AC supply of mains electricity forms a **sine wave**.

The current supplied to most homes is **single-phase** – it forms one sine wave. In factories and large buildings, which have powerful electrical equipment, the supply is often **three-phase** – effectively three currents, each with a different **phase** (timing). This provides a smoother supply as it reduces the gaps between the voltage peaks.

Note: The term **mains electricity** is not used in American English – terms like **supply** are used.

B AC generation and supply

Mains electricity is **generated** (produced) at sites called **power stations**, which use large **generators**. A generator converts mechanical energy to electrical energy. A generator rotates a magnet within an iron surround. The iron – called an **armature** – has coils of wire around it, called **field coils** (or **field windings**). As the magnet rotates, it causes current to flow through the field coils, due to **electromagnetic induction**.

Current from the generators leaves the power station and enters the **power grid** (or **grid**) – the network of **power lines** (cables) which transmit it around the country. At the point where it enters the grid, the electricity flows through **transformers** – specifically **step-up transformers**, which increase voltage and decrease amperage. This reduces the energy lost from the power lines over long distances, as **high-voltage (HV)** supplies flow more efficiently than **low-voltage (LV)** supplies. Before the supply is used by homes and other buildings, it passes through several **step-down transformers,** which reduce its voltage and increase its amperage.

The supply may be **stepped up** to over 400,000 volts at the point where it enters the large **transmission lines** (long-distance power lines) leaving the power station. It is normally then **stepped down** in stages, first passing through a wider network of lower-voltage transmission lines, and finally through the small **distribution lines** which supply streets and houses – in many countries at around 230 volts.

C DC generation and use

The extract below is from a consumer magazine.

Photovoltaic cells (PVs) – or solar cells – are an effective way of generating your own electricity from sunlight. The current they produce can be used immediately, may be stored in **rechargeable batteries** (like the ones in cars), or can be fed into the power grid and sold to the electric company. But PVs produce direct current. This is fine for **charging** batteries, but is not suitable for powering household appliances, which require alternating current. For this, the DC supply from PVs and batteries needs to go through an **inverter** – a device which converts DC to AC.

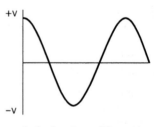

A single-phase AC supply

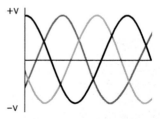

A three-phase AC supply

44.1 Complete the text about inverters using words from A opposite. Look at A, B and C opposite to help you.

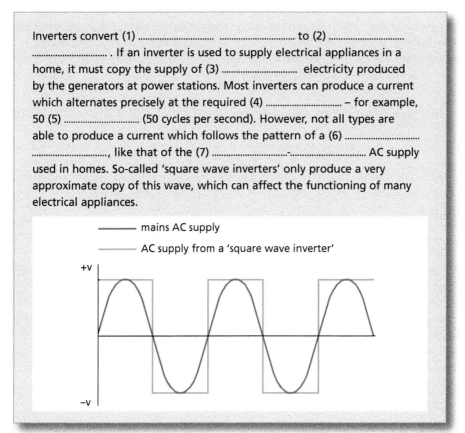

Inverters convert (1) .... to (2) ....
.... If an inverter is used to supply electrical appliances in a
home, it must copy the supply of (3) .... electricity produced
by the generators at power stations. Most inverters can produce a current
which alternates precisely at the required (4) .... – for example,
50 (5) .... (50 cycles per second). However, not all types are
able to produce a current which follows the pattern of a (6) ....
.............................., like that of the (7) .... -............................... AC supply
used in homes. So-called 'square wave inverters' only produce a very
approximate copy of this wave, which can affect the functioning of many
electrical appliances.

mains AC supply

AC supply from a 'square wave inverter'

44.2 Choose the correct words from the brackets to complete the descriptions of different stages
of AC generation and supply (a–f). Then, put the stages in the correct order. Look at B
opposite to help you.

a After the step-up transformer, the current enters a (distribution / transmission) line.
b Current is produced, by electromagnetic induction, in the (magnet / field coils) of a generator.
c The current goes from the last step-down transformer to a (distribution / transmission) line.
d The current leaves the power (grid / station) and enters the home.
e Amperage is reduced and voltage is increased by a (step-up / step-down) transformer.
f The current is stepped (up / down) from a higher voltage to a lower voltage, in stages.

44.3 Decide whether the sentences below are true or false, and correct the false sentences. Look at
A, B and C opposite to help you.

1 Photovoltaic cells produce direct current.
2 The electricity supply from PVs can be used to charge rechargeable batteries.
3 Rechargeable batteries supply electricity as alternating current.
4 Inverters convert sunlight to alternating current.

Over to you

Think of some large and small electrical appliances you're familiar with. Explain their
electrical supply requirements. What type of current is required, and how is it supplied and/
or converted?

45 Circuits and components

A Simple circuits

The circuit diagrams below show lamps connected in a **parallel circuit** and in a **series circuit**. The supply has **live** and **neutral** conductors. On an alternating current (AC) supply, the difference between live and neutral is that conductors on the neutral side of appliances are **earthed** – that is, connected to **earth** (the ground).

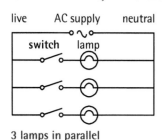

3 lamps in parallel

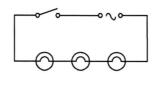

3 lamps in series

| BrE: live; AmE: phase |
| BrE: earth, earthed; AmE: ground, grounded |

B Mains AC circuits and switchboards

Where an AC supply enters a building, it is connected to a **switchboard**. This has a number of switches to allow different circuits in the building to be **switched on** and **off**. Circuits include **power circuits**. These supply the **power sockets** (or **sockets**) for the **plugs** on appliances. Usually, a **circuit-breaker** is fitted to each circuit. This is a safety switch that switches off automatically if there is a problem. This may happen if a person touches a live conductor, or if there is a **short circuit**. A short circuit is when current flows directly from a live conductor to a neutral conductor – for example, due to damaged insulation. Circuit breakers also allow circuits to be switched off manually, to **isolate** them (switch them off safely) – for example, before maintenance work.

Note: The equipment in **switchboards** is often called **switchgear**.

C Printed and integrated circuits

The circuits in electrical appliances are often **printed circuits**, on **printed circuit boards** (PCBs). These are **populated** with (fitted with) electrical components. Many appliances also contain small, complex **integrated circuits** – often called **microchips** (or **chips**) – made from silicon **wafers** (very thin pieces of silicon). They act as **semiconductors**, which can be positively charged at certain points on their surface and negatively charged at other points.
This principle is used to make very small circuits.

D Electrical and electronic components

There are many types of electrical and **electronic** components. These can be used individually or combined with other components to perform different tasks. For example:

- **Sensors** or **detectors** can **sense** or **detect** levels of – or changes in – values such as temperature, pressure and light.

- **Control systems** use feedback from sensors to control devices automatically. For example, mechanical devices such as water valves may be moved or adjusted by **servomechanisms** – electrically powered mechanisms that are controlled automatically by **signals** ('messages') from sensors.

- **Logic gates** are widely used in control systems. They send signals, in the form of low voltages, to other devices. An output signal from the logic gate is switched on or off, depending on the input signals it receives.

Notes: The term **electronic**, rather than **electrical**, generally describes small but often very complex circuits and components that operate at a low voltage.

See Appendix XII on page 114 for more on electrical and electronic components and logic gates, and Appendix XIII on page 118 for more on sensors and detectors.

45.1 Make word combinations with *circuit* using words from A and B opposite. Then match the combinations with the descriptions (1–6) below.

a ....
a ....
a ....   **circuit**
a ....
a ....
an ....

1 a circuit containing one or more sockets
2 a simple circuit where all the components are placed one after the other along the same conductor
3 a microchip – a very small, often complex circuit
4 what happens if live and neutral conductors touch while a current is flowing, and there is no component or appliance between them
5 a circuit which allows different components to be controlled independently by separate switches
6 a circuit that can be populated with a large number of components

45.2 Complete the task from an engineering textbook. Sometimes more than one word is possible. Look at B and C opposite and Appendix XIII on page 118 to help you.

> In an experiment, the lights in a room are connected to two types of electronic
> (1) .... The first is an occupancy sensor, which will (2) .... the
> movement of a person entering the room, and the second is some kind of photosensor, which
> can determine whether it's daylight or dark. These two devices are connected to an AND gate
> – a (3) .... that will produce an output current only if it receives
> two input currents – in this case, from both the occupancy sensor *and* the photosensor.
> Therefore, a (4) .... will be sent to the light switch to (5) ....
> .... the lights only if a person enters the room *and* if it's dark.
>
> However, for this system to work, we are assuming that the type of photosensor used will be
> one which is designed to produce a current in the dark, and which will then (6) ....
> .... as soon as daylight appears. But such a sensor may be designed to work in
> the opposite way – producing a current when it detects daylight and no current in the dark.
> This would cause an obvious problem. In this case, what type of logic gate could be placed
> between the photosensor and the AND gate in order to solve the problem?

45.3 Can you answer the question in the text in 45.2? Look at Appendix XIII on page 118 to help you.

A printed circuit board

An integrated circuit on a microchip

Over to you

Think of a device or installation you're familiar with which is automatically controlled, and describe its control systems. What kinds of sensor are used? How does the control system react to different signals from the sensors?

Three-dimensional drawings

An oblique projection shows an object with one of its faces at the front. The 3D shape of the object is shown by lines at 45 degrees from the horizontal.

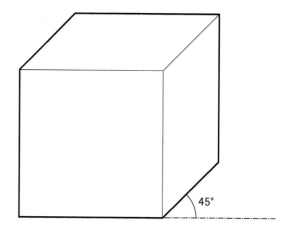

An oblique projection

An isometric projection shows an object with one of its corners at the front. The 3D shape of the object is shown by lines at 30 degrees from the horizontal.

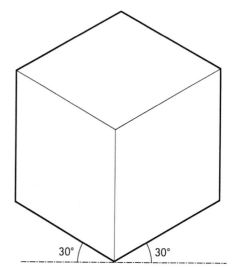

An isometric projection

An exploded view shows an assembly with its components spaced out, to show how the components fit together.

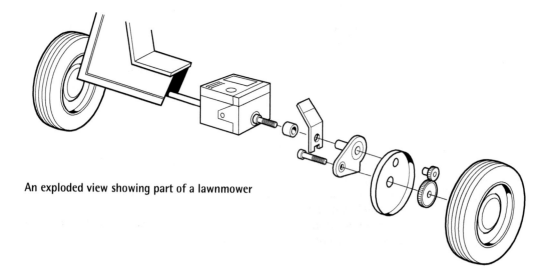

An exploded view showing part of a lawnmower

Appendix II Shapes

The nouns and adjectives below can be used to describe the shapes of components and assemblies.

2D shapes

Noun	Adjective	
square	square	□
rectangle	rectangular	▭
triangle	triangular	△
hexagon	hexagonal	⬡
octagon	octagonal	⯃
pentagon	pentagonal	⬠
circle	circular	○
semicircle	semicircular	◠
spiral	spiral	🌀

3D shapes

Noun	Adjective	
cube	cubic	
cylinder	cylindrical	
tube	tubular	
sphere	spherical	
hemisphere	hemispherical	
dome	dome-shaped	
cone	conical / cone-shaped	
pyramid	pyramidal / pyramid-shaped	
helix	helical	
wedge	wedge-shaped	

Notes: The noun **cylinder** is often used to describe a hollow cylinder that is enclosed – for example, piston cylinders (in engines) or gas cylinders (gas containers). A hollow cylinder that is open at both ends is generally called a **tube**.

The difference between a **dome** and a **hemisphere** is that a dome is hollow (not solid), and is not necessarily perfectly hemispherical.

In everyday English, **spiral** is often used to describe a **helix** – for example, a spiral staircase. The helical groove on a screw, bolt or nut is called a **thread**.

Units of measurement

SI base units

The **International System of Units** – abbreviated as **SI** from the French name, *Système International d'Unités* – is the most widely used system of measurements. Some **SI units**, such as metres and kilograms, are often described as **metric** units. The seven **base units** of the SI system are shown in the table below.

Quantity	Unit	Abbreviation
length	metre	m
mass	kilogram	kg
time	second	s
electric current	ampere	A
thermodynamic temperature	kelvin	K
amount of substance	mole	mol
luminous intensity	candela	cd

Note: 0 kelvin (K) = –273 degrees Celsius (°C). 0 K is the lowest possible temperature – often called absolute zero.

SI derived units

SI derived units are related to the SI base units. They include a wide range of specific units. The table below lists SI derived units commonly used in engineering.

Quantity	Unit	Abbreviation	Notes
length	millimetre	mm	$1\,mm = 0.001\,m$
	centimetre	cm	$1\,cm = 0.01\,m$
	kilometre	km	$1\,km = 1{,}000\,m$
area	square metre	m²	$1\,m^2 = 1\,m \times 1\,m$
	square millimetre	mm²	$1\,mm^2 = 1\,mm \times 1\,mm$
volume	cubic metre	m³	$1\,m^3 = 1\,m \times 1\,m \times 1\,m$
	cubic centimetre	cc	$1\,cc = 1\,cm \times 1\,cm \times 1\,cm$
volume of liquid	litre	l	$1\,l = 0.001\,m^3$
mass	gram	g	$1\,g = 0.001\,kg$
	tonne	T	$1\,T = 1{,}000\,kg$
force	newton	N	$1\,N$ = the force exerted by the earth's gravity on a mass of approximately $0.1\,kg$
density	kilograms per cubic metre	kg/m³	If a volume of $1\,m^3$ of material has a mass of $1\,kg$ its density = $1\,kg/m^3$.
pressure and stress	Pascal	Pa	$1\,Pa = 1\,N/m^2$

Quantity	Unit	Abbreviation	Notes
speed/velocity	metres per second	m/s	If an object travels 1 metre in 1 second, its speed or velocity is 1 m/s.
	kilometres per hour	km/h	If an object travels 1 kilometre in 1 hour, its speed or velocity is 1 km/h.
acceleration	metres per second squared	m/s^2	If the speed or velocity of an object increases by 1 m/s every second, it has a rate of acceleration of 1 m/s^2.
moments and torque	newton metres	Nm	1 Nm = 1 N of force exerted at a distance of 1 m from a fulcrum or axis of rotation
temperature	degree Celsius	°C	Temperature in °C = temperature in kelvin (K) + 273 (see note under base units above)
frequency	hertz	Hz	1 Hz = 1 cycle per second
angular movement	radian	rad	2π rad = 360 degrees
angular velocity	radians per second	rad/s	If an object rotates through 1 radian in 1 second, its angular velocity is 1 rad/s.
angular acceleration	radians per second squared	rad/s^2	If the angular velocity of an object increases by 1 rad/s every second, its angular acceleration is 1 rad/s^2.
rotational velocity	revolutions per minute	rpm	If a revolving shaft or wheel makes 1,000 rotations every minute, its rotational velocity is 1,000 rpm.
energy	joule	J	If a force of 1 N is needed to keep an object moving, the work required to move the object over 1 m = 1 J.
power	watt	W	1 W = 1 J/s
specific heat capacity	joules per kilogram degrees Celsius	J/(kg °C)	If 1 J of energy is needed to raise the temperature of 1 kg of a substance by 1°C, its specific heat capacity is 1 J/(kg °C).
latent heat of fusion and latent heat of vaporization	joules per kilogram	J/kg	If 1 J of energy is needed to change the state of 1 kg of a substance, its latent heat of fusion/vaporization is 1 J/kg.

SI units for electricity

	Unit	Abbreviation
electromotive force	volt	V
electrical resistance	ohm	Ω
electrical conductance	siemens	S
electrical charge	coulomb	C
capacitance	farad	F
inductance	henry	H
magnetic flux	weber	Wb
magnetic flux density	tesla	T

Unit prefixes

The prefixes below can be written in front of units to multiply them or divide them by a specific number. For example, 1 **milliamp** (**mA**) = 0.001 amps, and 1 **kilonewton** (**kN**) = 1,000 newtons.

Prefix	Abbreviation	Multiplication factor
tera	T	× 1,000,000,000,000
giga	G	× 1,000,000,000
mega	M	× 1,000,000
kilo	k	× 1,000
hecto	h	× 100
deka	da	× 10
deci	d	× 0.1
centi	c	× 0.01
milli	m	× 0.001
micro	μ	× 0.000001
nano	n	× 0.000000001
pico	p	× 0.000000000001

Common UK Imperial, US Customary and other non-SI units

Quantity	Unit	Abbreviation	Description	SI equivalent
length	inch (plural, inches)	in		1 in = 25.4 mm
	foot (plural, feet)	ft	12 in	1 ft = 304.8 mm
	yard	yd	3 ft	1 yd = 914.4 mm
	statute mile (or mile)	(no standard)	5,280 ft	1 statute mile = 1,609.344 m

Quantity	Unit	Abbreviation	Description	SI equivalent
length	nautical mile (used in aviation and shipping)	(no standard)	6,076.115 ft	1 nautical mile = 1,852 m
speed/velocity	miles per hour (statute miles per hour)	mph	miles travelled in 1 hour	1 mph = 1.609344 km/h
	knot (nautical miles per hour)	kn / kt(s)	nautical miles travelled in 1 hour	1 kt = 1.852 km/h
mass	ounce (international avoirdupois ounce)	oz		1 oz = 0.02835 kg
	pound (international avoirdupois pound)	lb	16 oz	1 lb = 0.45359237 kg
pressure and stress	pound-force per square inch	psi		1 psi = 6,894.76 Pa
atmospheric pressure	bar		approximately equal to atmospheric pressure at sea level	1 bar = 100,000 Pa
torque	foot-pound force (foot pounds)	ft.lb	moment of 1 lb force exerted at 1 ft from a shaft's axis of rotation	approx. 1.35581 Nm
engine power	mechanical horsepower	hp	a historic unit	approx. 745.7 W
	metric horsepower	hp	a historic unit	approx. 735.5 W

Notes: In British industry, SI units – not imperial units – are used.

In aviation and shipping, nautical miles (distance), knots (speed) and feet (altitude – for aircraft) are used as the international standard.

Engine horsepower is usually measured in **brake horsepower (bhp)**. This is the power of the engine measured at the engine's output shaft. The word 'brake' comes from the technique used to measure engine power in the past. In power tests, a brake was applied to the output shaft to resist the torque of the engine. The amount of braking force required to do this was measured.

Degrees Fahrenheit

The following calculations can be used to convert **degrees Fahrenheit** (°F) to degrees Celsius (°C), and vice versa:

°C = (°F − 32) × 5/9

°F = (°C × 9/5) + 32

Appendix IV Chemical elements

Element	Symbol	Element	Symbol
actinium	Ac	fermium	Fm
aluminium (BrE) / aluminum (AmE)	Al	fluorine	F
americium	Am	francium	Fr
antimony	Sb	gadolinium	Gd
argon	Ar	gallium	Ga
arsenic	As	germanium	Ge
astatine	At	gold	Au
barium	Ba	hafnium	Hf
berkelium	Bk	hassium	Hs
beryllium	Be	helium	He
bismuth	Bi	holmium	Ho
bohrium	Bh	hydrogen	H
boron	B	indium	In
bromine	Br	iodine	I
cadmium	Cd	iridium	Ir
caesium (BrE) / cesium (AmE)	Cs	iron	Fe
calcium	Ca	krypton	Kr
californium	Cf	lanthanum	La
carbon	C	lawrencium	Lr
cerium	Ce	lead	Pb
chlorine	Cl	lithium	Li
chromium	Cr	lutetium	Lu
cobalt	Co	magnesium	Mg
copper	Cu	manganese	Mn
curium	Cm	meitnerium	Mt
darmstadtium	Ds	mendelevium	Md
dubnium	Db	mercury	Hg
dysprosium	Dy	molybdenum	Mo
einsteinium	Es	neodymium	Nd
erbium	Er	neon	Ne
europium	Eu	neptunium	Np

Element	Symbol
nickel	Ni
niobium	Nb
nitrogen	N
nobelium	No
osmium	Os
oxygen	O
palladium	Pd
phosphorus	P
platinum	Pt
plutonium	Pu
polonium	Po
potassium	K
praseodymium	Pr
promethium	Pm
protactinium	Pa
radium	Ra
radon	Rn
rhenium	Re
rhodium	Rh
roentgenium	Rg
rubidium	Rb
ruthenium	Ru
rutherfordium	Rf
samarium	Sm
scandium	Sc
seaborgium	Sg
selenium	Se
silicon	Si
silver	Ag
sodium	Na
strontium	Sr

Element	Symbol
sulphur (BrE) / sulfur (AmE)	S
tantalum	Ta
technetium	Tc
tellurium	Te
terbium	Tb
thallium	Tl
thorium	Th
thulium	Tm
tin	Sn
titanium	Ti
tungsten	W
uranium	U
vanadium	V
xenon	Xe
ytterbium	Yb
yttrium	Y
zinc	Zn
zirconium	Zr

Appendix V
Structural elements and types of load

Common structural elements

The table below lists the structural elements commonly found in large structures, in:

- the **substructure** – elements situated below **ground level** (below the ground)
- the **superstructure** – elements situated above ground level.

Element	Description
foundation	an element in the ground, usually made of concrete, which transmits loads from a structure to the soil or rocks in the ground below it
pad foundation	a square foundation – usually supports a column
strip foundation	a long, narrow foundation – usually supports a wall
raft foundation	a large rectangular foundation which covers the entire area of the building that it supports – effectively a thick slab which acts as a foundation
pile	a vertical column of concrete below the ground which provides a strong foundation – may be cast in-situ by pouring concrete into a hole that has been **bored** (drilled), or may be precast and **driven** (hammered) into the ground
pile cap	a block of concrete, at ground level, built directly on top of a pile or **pile cluster** (several piles close together) to provide a flat foundation – for a column, for example
ground beam	a concrete beam at ground level which connects two pile caps – pile foundations often consist of a network of ground beams connecting a number of pile caps
basement	one or more floors of a building situated below ground level, surrounded by walls
retaining wall	a wall which supports earth behind it, allowing the ground behind it to be at a higher level than the ground in front of it – the wall **retains** the earth (holds it back)
column	a vertical structural element with a relatively small cross-section – in large structures, often consists of reinforced concrete, a steel Universal Column (UC), or an **encased** UC – that is, a UC **encased in** (surrounded by) concrete
beam	a horizontal structural element with a relatively small cross-section – in large structures, often consists of reinforced concrete or a steel Universal Beam (UB) – frequently spans between two columns
slab	an area of concrete generally with a constant thickness, most often a **floor slab** (a slab for a floor) – called a **suspended slab** if it spans between supporting beams, including ground beams
dam	a wall which holds back water behind it – for example, across a valley to **dam** a river and create a **reservoir** (a manmade lake)

Note: See Unit 16 for more on in-situ concrete and precast concrete.

Structural sections

universal beam (UB) an I-section with a depth greater than its width	I-section (depth greater than width)
universal column (UC) an I-section whose outside dimensions are roughly square	I-section (roughly square)
rolled steel joist (RSJ) a term sometimes used to refer to I-sections generally	I-section
rolled steel channel (RSC) a C-section	C-section
rolled steel angle (RSA) an L-section	L-section
structural tee a T-section	T-section
circular hollow section (CHS) a circular tube	circle
rectangular hollow section (RHS) a square or rectangular tube	rectangle

Types of load

Type of load	Description	Examples
dead load	a load that never changes, such as the **self-weight** of a structure (its own weight)	the weight of the concrete from which a bridge is built
live load	a load whose magnitude can be different at different times – usually **imposed on** (put on) a machine or structure by something that is not part of the machine or structure	cargo carried by a truck – different weights of cargo may be carried on different trips
static load	a load that remains still (does not move)	the dead load of a building, or a live load which remains still, such as snow lying on a roof
dynamic load	a moving load, such as one which produces a sudden shock but lasts for only a brief moment (an **impulse**)	aircraft wheels hitting the runway on landing
point load	a load which is **concentrated** – that is, one which acts on a small area	the end of a set screw pressing on a shaft (see Unit 27)
uniformly distributed load (UDL)	a load which is spread evenly over a reasonably large area	the weight of water acting on the bottom of a swimming pool

The diagrams show how the load supported or lifted can be increased by moving the effort further from the fulcrum. In both diagrams, the **clockwise moment** – the force turning the lever in the same direction as the hands of a clock – is equal to the **anticlockwise moment**. The levers are therefore in equilibrium (see Unit 32). In order to lift the load, the clockwise turning moment would need to be increased slightly.

Lever 1

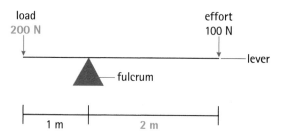

Clockwise moment: 100 N x 2 m = 200 Nm
Anticlockwise moment: 200 N x 1 m = 200 Nm

Lever 2

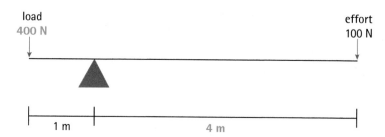

Clockwise moment: 100 N x 4 m = 400 Nm
Anticlockwise moment: 400 N x 1 m = 400 Nm

Vapour, cooling and thermal inertia

Gas and vapour

A gas can also be called a **vapour** – for example, **water vapour**. The definition of a vapour is a gas which is below its critical temperature. This means the gas can be condensed by putting it under pressure. Above the critical temperature (374 °C in the case of water), the gas can no longer be condensed by pressure.

Steam

Water vapour is often called **steam**. When it is extremely hot – such as in electricity-generating turbines – it is called **superheated steam**.

Cooling and thermal inertia

Radiators are widely used in **cooling systems** – for example, in vehicle engines. Liquid – called **coolant** – is pumped around the hot engine to absorb heat, and travels through a radiator positioned at the front of the vehicle. As the vehicle moves, air flows over the radiator. The **airflow** cools the radiator and the coolant inside it. Without a cooling system, the engine would **overheat**. However, this would not happen immediately after starting the engine, due to **thermal inertia** – the fact that it takes time to change the temperature of a heavy mass of material (such as an engine), either when it is heated or cooled. An object with a high level of thermal inertia can be described as a **heat sink**.

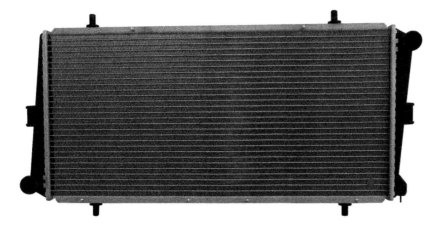

A radiator for an engine cooling system

The electromagnetic spectrum

The diagram below shows the types of wave in the electromagnetic spectrum.

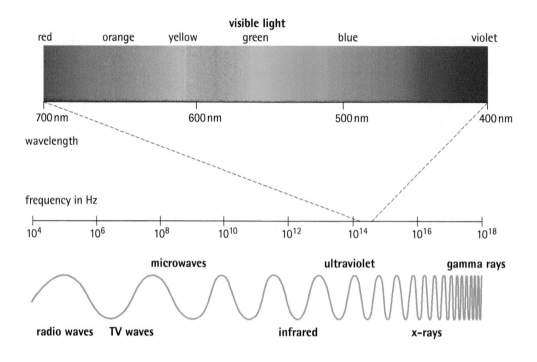

nm = nanometres

Appendix IX

Pipe and hose fittings and valves

Pipe and hose fittings

a ninety-degree elbow

a forty five-degree elbow

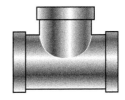

a tee

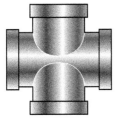

a cross

a union

a flange: allows larger pipes to be bolted together, end to end

a plug: fits inside the end of a pipe to close it

a cap: fits over the outside of the end of a pipe to close it

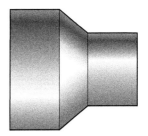

a reducer: allows two pipes of different diameters to be connected

Valves

The flow of liquid through pipes and hoses can be controlled by **valves**. According to their type, these devices can:

- be fully opened to allow a flow, or fully closed to **shut off** (stop) the flow
- be partly opened/closed to **regulate** the **flow rate** (control the volume of flow)
- **direct the flow**, by allowing it to go along one pipe or another at a junction
- provide an **inlet**, allowing liquid or gas to enter a pipe or tank, or an **outlet**, allowing liquid or gas to exit
- act as a **safety valve** in a pressure vessel, allowing gas to escape if a dangerously high pressure is reached, to prevent an explosion
- act as a **check valve** (or **non-return valve**), allowing liquid or gas to flow in only one direction.

Siphonic action

Hydrostatic pressure allows liquids to be **siphoned**. The principle of **siphonic action** can be shown using a hose – called a **siphon** in this situation – to make liquid flow upwards from its **surface level,** over the side of a tank and then downwards. The hose must first be **primed** – that is, completely filled with water. The top end of the hose must then be **immersed** in the liquid (put below the surface). The bottom end may also be immersed, although this is not necessary. When the flow begins, the liquid in the hose must run **at full bore** – that is, the **bore** of the hose (its inside diameter) must be completely filled with water, with no air in it.

Siphonic action is often used to drain rainwater from the roofs of large buildings. Unlike normal rainwater pipes, the pipes of **siphonic drainage** systems are designed to run at full bore, which allows them to flow much faster. This means smaller-diameter pipes can be used. These take up less space in the building.

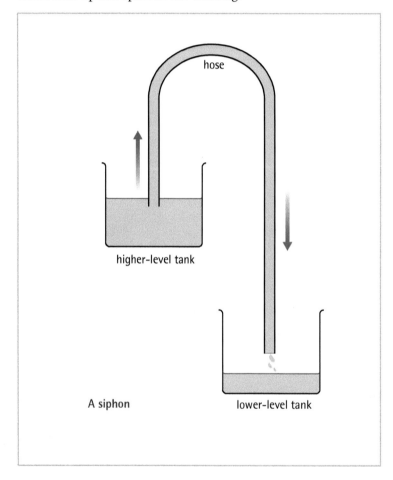

hose

higher-level tank

A siphon   lower-level tank

Managing rotary motion

The following mechanisms are often used in machines that have rotating shafts and wheels.

Mechanism	Notes
a **bearing**	■ allows a shaft, such as a driveshaft or an **axle** (a shaft to which a vehicle's wheels are fixed) to revolve inside a hole ■ may require a **lubricant** – oil or **grease** – to help reduce friction
a **universal joint**	■ used to connect the ends of two shafts that are at an angle to each other, allowing drive to be transmitted, through the angle, between the two shafts
a **clutch**	■ allows drive to be transmitted progressively (by friction), from a constantly revolving driveshaft, to wheels that are not yet revolving ■ may be operated manually, or may be an automatically operated **centrifugal clutch**
brakes	■ used to slow down and stop rotary motion, usually by friction ■ in **disc brakes**, a pair of **brake pads** is pressed against the sides of a metal **brake disc** which is fixed to the shaft ■ in **drum brakes**, brake pads are pressed against the inside of a hollow cylinder, called a **drum**

A universal joint

Electrical and electronic components

Common components and their functions

Component	Function
amplifier	**amplifies** an electric current – that is, increases the **amplitude** (wave height) of the current
antenna	**receives** or **transmits** (sends) radio signals
battery	several cells connected together
capacitor	consists of two conductors which are separated by a **dielectric** (insulating) material – allows a certain amount of electrical charge to be stored
cell	an electrical storage device, containing chemicals, which supplies a direct current
circuit-breaker	a safety device which automatically switches off a circuit
diode	a device with two terminals which allows current to flow in one direction only
fuse	a thin conductor which burns and breaks at a certain amperage, to protect a circuit
inductor	a coil which is used to produce electromagnetic induction
inverter	converts direct current to alternating current
lamp	produces light – often an **incandescent lamp**, which consists of a filament inside a glass bulb
potentiometer	a variable resistor with three connections
rectifier	converts alternating current to direct current
relay	a switch which is operated electrically (not mechanically)
resistor	produces a precise amount of resistance
rheostat	a variable resistor with two terminals
speaker / loudspeaker	converts electrical energy to sound energy
switch	allows electric current to flow when closed (**switched on**), and stops current flowing when opened (**switched off**)
transformer	a **step-up transformer** increases voltage and reduces amperage, and a **step-down transformer** reduces voltage and increases amperage
transistor	a device with three terminals which can be used as an amplifier or switch

Components and symbols

Component	Symbol	Component	Symbol
ammeter		Schottky diode	
amplifier		tunnel diode	
antenna		Zener diode	
battery		fuse	
capacitors		inductors	
fixed capacitor		air-core inductor	
feed-through capacitor		bifilar inductor	
polarized capacitor		iron-core inductor	
variable capacitor		tapped inductor	
cell		variable inductor	
circuit-breaker		lamp	
delay line		microphone	
diodes		motor	
Gunn diode		ohmmeter	
light-emitting diode (LED)		oscilloscope	
PIN diode		piezoelectric crystal	
photodiode			

Component	Symbol		Component	Symbol
resistors			rotary switch	
fixed resistor			**transformers**	
variable resistor (rheostat)			air-core transformer	
speaker / loudspeaker			iron-core transformer	
switches			**transistors**	
single pole, single throw (SPST) switch			bipolar NPN (negative, positive, negative) transistor	
single pole, double throw (SPDT) switch			bipolar PNP (positive, negative, positive) transistor	
double pole, single throw (DPST) switch			field-effect N-channel (negative channel) transistor	
double pole, double throw (DPDT) switch			field-effect P-channel (positive channel) transistor	
momentary contact switch, normally open (NO) / push-to-make switch			MOS (metal oxide semiconductor) field-effect N-channel transistor	
momentary contact switch, normally closed (NC) / push-to-break switch			MOS field-effect P-channel transistor	
			voltmeter	
			wattmeter	

Logic gates

Logic gates are electronic devices generally made from transistors and diodes. All types of logic gate, except NOT gates (see below), have two input terminals. The input terminals receive signals in the form of voltages, and are designed to simply detect whether there is a voltage (considered to be the signal '1'), or not (considered to be the signal '0').

All logic gates have one output terminal, which can send the signal 1 (a voltage) or the signal 0 (no voltage). Whether the logic gate sends a 1 or a 0 depends on the combination of signals received by the input terminals, and on the type of logic gate being used. The different types of logic gate are shown below.

AND gate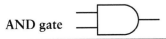

Input 1	Input 2	Output
0	0	0
0	1	0
1	0	0
1	1	1

The output signal is 1 only if both input signals are 1.

NOT gate, or inverter

Input 1	Input 2
1	0
0	1

The gate only has one input point. The output signal is the opposite of the input signal.

OR gate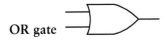

Input 1	Input 2	Output
0	0	0
0	1	1
1	0	1
1	1	1

The output signal is 1 if (a) either one of the input signals is 1, or if (b) both input signals are 1.

XOR gate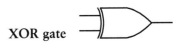

Input 1	Input 2	Output
0	0	0
0	1	1
1	0	1
1	1	0

The output signal is 1 if either of the input signals is 1, but is 0 if both input signals are 1.

NAND gate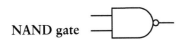

Input 1	Input 2	Output
0	0	1
0	1	1
1	0	1
1	1	0

A NAND gate is the opposite of an AND gate, functioning as an AND gate + a NOT gate.

NOR gate

Input 1	Input 2	Output
0	0	1
0	1	0
1	0	0
1	1	0

A NOR gate is the opposite of an OR gate, functioning as an OR gate + a NOT gate.

XNOR gate

Input 1	Input 2	Output
0	0	1
0	1	0
1	0	0
1	1	1

An XNOR gate is the opposite of an XOR gate, functioning as an XOR gate + a NOT gate.

Sensing, measuring and regulating devices

Device	Function
voltmeter	detects and measures voltage
ammeter	detects and measures electric current
ohmmeter	detects and measures electrical resistance
thermostat	regulates temperature – switches a heating or cooling system on or off at a set temperature
thermocouple	measures or controls temperature – produces a voltage which varies proportionally as the temperature difference between two points varies
thermistor	measures or controls temperature – produces a resistance which varies proportionally as temperature varies (thermistor is short for 'thermal resistor')
photosensor	a general term for devices that detect and measure light
proximity sensor	measures the distance between itself and nearby objects
piezoelectric sensor	measures movement and strain – produces an electric current when stressed mechanically
flowmeter	measures the rate of flow of a fluid
barometer	measures atmospheric pressure
hygrometer	measures the amount of moisture (water vapour) in the air
altimeter	measures altitude, usually as a height above sea level
smoke detector	detects smoke, usually to provide a fire warning
accelerometer	measures acceleration and deceleration forces
motion detector	detects movement – usually of people – that are a certain distance away
microphone	detects sound

A smoke detector

A digital **multimeter** can measure amperage and voltage.

Answer key

1.1 1 actual size 3 general arrangement 5 set
         2 scale   4 schematics   6 CAD

1.2 1f, 2b, 3a, 4e, 5d, 6c

1.3 1 general arrangement   3 drawing   5 cross-section
         2 computer-aided design 4 three-dimensional 6 one to fifty

1.4 1 section   3 plan   5 3D   7 scale
         2 GA   4 elevation 6 schematic   8 detail

2.1 1 design brief   3 preliminary drawing
         2 sketch   4 concept

2.2 1 amend, redesign, refine, revise   3 approve, sign off
         2 circulate, issue   4 supersede

2.3 1 draft   3 work   5 working
         2 current 4 comment

2.4 1 issued   3 notes   5 draft   7 current
         2 revision 4 amendments 6 superseded 8 work

3.1 1 constraint, budget, exceed   3 function, designed, feature
         2 cost-effective   4 existing, proposed

3.2 1 determined   4 overdesigned
         2 worst-case scenarios 5 belt and braces
         3 factored in   6 Sizing

3.3 1 allow for   3 overdesigning 5 worst-case scenarios
         2 factor of safety 4 quantify   6 cost-effective

4.1 1 overall 3 height 5 thickness
         2 span   4 width

4.2 1 false – The height of the towers is measured <u>vertically</u>.
         2 false – The overall span is measured along the <u>length</u> of the bridge.
         3 true
         4 true
         5 false – The thickness of each tower decreases towards the top, so the faces of the towers
           are <u>out of plumb</u>.
         6 false – The greatest thickness of each tower is its <u>external</u> thickness at its base.

4.3 2 plumb   4 out of plumb   6 height
         3 inclined 5 length

4.4 The towers are plumb, but because they are
         a long distance apart, the curvature of the
         earth (the curve of the earth's surface) has a
         noticeable effect, which is increased by the
         height of the towers. The diagram below
         shows the effect in exaggerated form.

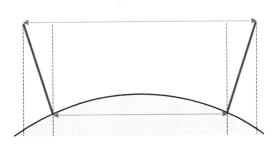

5.1
1 at 175 mm centres
2 centreline
3 offset
4 at a right-angle / at right-angles
5 locate

5.2
1 gridline
2 set out
3 parallel
4 intersect
5 perpendicular
6 square off

5.3 1b, 2a, 3d, 4c

6.1
1 circular
2 radius
3 diameter
4 circumference
5 constant
6 arc
7 deformed
8 curved
9 chord

6.2
1 the crown
2 the invert
3 the outside diameter
4 the inside diameter / the bore

6.3
1 The distance travelled by the vehicle each time its wheels turn completely is equal to the circumference of one of its tyres.
2 The radius of the tyre is measured from the centre of the wheel to the outside edge of the tyre.
3 The radius of the curve in the motorway is constant, so the edges of the road follow arcs of a circle.
4 The curve in the motorway has a constant radius, so the inside and outside edges of the road are arcs of two concentric circles that have the same centre.
5 The crown is on the circumference of the external face of the pipe, and therefore cannot be in contact with the liquid flowing inside the pipe.
6 The thickness of the wall at the bottom of the pipe, plus the distance between the invert and the crown of the pipe, is equal to the outside diameter of the pipe.

7.1
1 permissible
2 accurate / precise
3 vary / deviate
4 precision / accuracy
5 imprecise / inaccurate
6 variation / range
7 within tolerance
8 outside tolerance
9 tight tolerance / close tolerance
10 loose tolerance

7.2 1b, 2f, 3e, 4c, 5a, 6d

7.3
1 variation
2 precise
3 tolerances
4 plus
5 minus
6 within
7 permissible
8 range
9 fit
10 clearances

8.1
1 one point seven nine three
2 a/one hundredth of a
3 a/one thousandth of a
4 zero, nought

8.2
1 fraction
2 rounded up, decimal places
3 rounded down, decimal place
4 whole
5 negligible
6 rounding error

8.3
1 plus
2 times
3 multiplied
4 divided
5 sum
6 square
7 subtract
8 square root
9 squared
10 less / minus

8.4
1 sum
2 square, multiplied by / times
3 multiplied by / times, divided by
4 square root
5 equal

9.1
1 density
2 cross-sectional area
3 volume
4 mass
5 surface area

9.2
1 metres
2 millimetres
3 square millimetres
4 square metres
5 cubic metres
6 kilograms
7 kilograms per cubic metre

9.3
1 cubic
2 mass
3 gravity
4 weigh
5 lightweight
6 weightless
7 square

10.1
1 consumption
2 consume
3 average
4 duration
5 constant
6 rate
7 cumulative
8 capacity

10.2
1 1, 7
2 4
3 7
4 9
5 2

10.3
1 output, supply, efficient
2 surplus, peak
3 gain

11.1
1 non-metal
2 non-ferrous
3 metal
4 ferrous
5 non-metallic
6 metallic

11.2
1 true
2 false – Alloys are <u>mixtures</u>, not compounds.
3 true
4 false – An alloying metal describes a metal added in a relatively <u>small</u> quantity.
5 false – Steel is not a single element. It is an <u>alloy</u>, consisting mainly of the elements iron and carbon.

11.3
1 Reinforced
2 reinforce
3 reinforcement
4 reinforcing/reinforcement
5 reinforced (aluminium-reinforced)

11.4
Elements: oxygen, iron
Compounds: water, iron oxide
Alloy: steel
Composite: reinforced concrete

12.1
1 true
2 false – Mild steel is a <u>low</u> carbon steel.
3 true
4 true
5 false – Low alloy steels contain <u>90% or more</u> iron, <u>and up to 10%</u> of alloying metals such as chromium.
6 true
7 false – Tungsten is added to steel to make it <u>harder</u>.
8 true

12.2

Verb	Noun	Adjective
corrode	corrosion	corroded
oxidize	oxide	oxidized
rust / go rusty	rust	rusty

1 corrodes / oxidizes / rusts / goes rusty
2 corrosion / oxide / rust
3 corroded / oxidized / rusty

12.3
1 steel
2 corrodes / oxidizes / rusts
3 grade
4 corrosion / oxidizing / rusting
5 stainless
6 chromium
7 rusty
8 corrosion / oxide / rust
9 iron

13.1
2 Titanium has a high strength-to-weight ratio and is often alloyed with aluminium.
3 Zinc can be mixed with copper to make brass.
4 Copper can be mixed with tin and lead to produce bronze.
5 Gold resists corrosion better than the other precious metal, silver.

13.2
Metal elements: copper, silver, titanium, zinc, aluminium, gold, tin, lead, magnesium
Alloys: duralumin, brass, bronze
Precious metals: silver, gold

13.3
1 electrolyte
2 plated
3 negative
4 electroplating
5 cathode
6 galvanizing
7 positive
8 anode

14.1
1 natural
2 manmade
3 atoms
4 molecules

14.2
1 true
2 true
3 false – The plastic is <u>solid</u>.
4 false – The tests check that the plastic <u>does not stretch</u> – an elastomer would stretch significantly.
5 true
6 false – Material is melted down and reused, something <u>not possible</u> with thermosetting plastics.
7 true

14.3

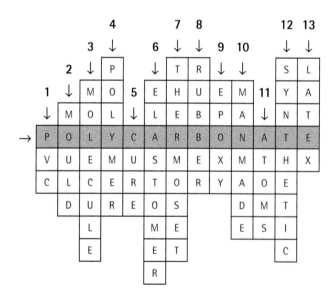

15.1
1 false – Minerals are <u>inorganic</u>.
2 true
3 true
4 true
5 false – Industrial diamond is an abrasive, <u>non-metallic</u> material.
6 false – In order to become ceramics, materials must be <u>heated/fired</u>. (Only glass-like ceramics are vitrified.)
7 true

15.2
1 laminated glass, safety glass, windscreen
2 safety glass, tempered glass, toughened glass
3 annealed glass

15.3
1 layers/sheets
2 laminated
3 bonding
4 toughened/tempered
5 shatter
6 layers/sheets

16.1
1 coarse aggregate
2 fine aggregate
3 cement
4 batching
5 mix design
6 28-day strength
7 water–cement ratio
8 additives
9 retarder
10 plasticizer

16.2
1 prestressing
2 reinforcement
3 pouring
4 precast
5 in-situ
6 formwork
7 cast
8 structural
9 concrete

17.1
1 c, e, f
2 a, f
3 c, d, f

17.2
1 planed
2 rough-sawn
3 stress grade
4 visually stress-graded
5 mechanically stress-graded

17.3
1 softwood / timber
2 stress-graded
3 glue-laminated
4 plywood
5 orientated strand board / OSB
6 particle
7 medium-density fibreboard / MDF

18.1
1 tension
2 compression
3 elongation
4 elongation, extension
5 deformation

18.2
1c, 2b, 3a, 4f, 5e, 6d

18.3
1 elastic
2 ductile
3 elastic limit
4 yield point
5 extension/elongation/deformation
6 plastically
7 elastically

19.1
1 indentation
2 abrasion
3 scratch
4 durability

19.2
1b, 2c, 3d, 4a

19.3
1 conduct
2 thermal conductivity
3 thermal conductor
4 expand
5 contract
6 expansion/contraction
7 contraction/expansion
8 coefficient of thermal expansion

20.1   1 casting: molten metal, heat, pressure, a die
2 sintering: metal powder, heat, pressure, a die
3 extrusion: molten metal, heat, pressure, a die

20.2   1 false – Metal can also be <u>cold forged</u>.
2 true
3 true
4 true
5 false – Metal can also be <u>cold rolled</u>.
6 true
7 false – Metal can also be work hardened by <u>cold forging</u>.
8 false – Shot-peening is a <u>cold forging</u> technique.

20.3   2 When metal is annealed, its temperature is allowed to decrease gradually in order to make it more elastic and less brittle.
3 If metal is quenched, this means its temperature is reduced rapidly, making it harder, but more brittle.
4 When a metal is tempered, it is held at a high temperature for a time, to improve its hardness without reducing its elasticity too much.
5 If a metal is case hardened, it is heated within a gas to harden only the metal near the surface.

20.4   1 extrusion   4 quenched
2 drop forged / hot forged   5 shot-peened
3 work hardened

21.1   1 true
2 true
3 false – Pellets are intended for <u>melting and forming in moulds</u>.
4 true
5 false – Steel <u>blooms</u> can be cut into smaller sized pieces called <u>billets</u>.

21.2   1 a steel bloom   5 a round bar, a rod   9 a steel wire
2 a coil of steel sheet   6 a flat bar   10 an electrical cable
3 a round PVC tube   7 a sheet of glass   11 a stranded wire
4 an aluminium plate   8 a steel cable   12 a solid wire

22.1   1c blind, 2e chamfered, 3d pointed, 4a groove, 5b flush

22.2   1 tapered   5 accommodate   9 recessed   13 ridge
2 tip   6 slot   10 flush   14 rounded
3 groove   7 chamfered   11 constant
4 square   8 countersunk   12 threaded

23.1   1c, 2d, 3e, 4f, 5b, 6a

23.2   1 a drill bit for metal
2 a holesaw
3 a blade for a hacksaw
4 a toothed blade for a circular saw
5 a thick abrasive wheel for a grinder
6 cores of concrete being removed by diamond drilling

23.3   1 turn   2 drill   3 saw   4 grind   5 mill

24.1   1 a, c, e   2 a, b   3 a, c, d   4 a, c, d, e

24.2
1 acetylene
2 oxygen
3 oxyacetylene
4 flame-cutting
5 ultra-high-pressure
6 edge quality
7 secondary operations

24.3
1 electrical discharge machining
2 spark erosion
3 a torch
4 an electric arc
5 It needs to be partly ionized.
6 a laser beam
7 heat-affected zone (HAZ)

25.1
1 supported
2 anchored
3 embedded
4 connection/joint
5 attached/connected/fastened/fixed/joined
6 together

25.2 1d, 2e, 3a, 4b, 5c

26.1
1 <u>Bolts</u> are well-known examples of fasteners.
2 In most cases, nuts are screwed onto bolts by turning them <u>clockwise</u>.
3 The threaded part of a bolt is the <u>shaft/shank</u>.
4 Threads are cut to form a <u>helical</u> pattern.
5 Allen keys are designed to fit <u>into</u> the heads of bolts.

26.2
1 tighten
2 preload
3 work loose
4 over-tighten
5 torque
6 tension
7 shear force
8 loosen

26.3
1 false – The purpose of <u>flat washers</u> and <u>plain washers</u> is to spread the load.
2 true
3 true
4 false – Spring washers allow the amount of preload to be <u>adjusted</u>.
5 false – Spring washers allow <u>some</u> movement to occur.

27.1
1 machine
2 self-tapping
3 slot head
4 crosshead
5 set/grub

27.2
1 plug
2 screw
3 screwdriver
4 expand
5 crosshead
6 head
7 pullout
8 set in

27.3 1e, 2d, 3a, 4c, 5b

28.1
1 welded together
2 dissimilar materials
3 base metal
4 molten
5 weld pool
6 fuse
7 discontinuities
8 weld zone
9 residual stresses
10 heat-affected zone

28.2 1 b, e   2 a, d, g, h   3 b, f   4 c, d, f

28.3 1e, 2f, 3h, 4c, 5a, 6g

29.1   1 spot welding   2 seam welding   3 ultrasonic welding   4 resistance welding

29.2
1 soft soldering, hard soldering, brazing
2 soft soldering
3 hard soldering
4 none
5 brazing, hard soldering
6 soft soldering
7 none

29.3
1 adhesive
2 adhere to
3 chemical bond
4 contact adhesive
5 substrate
6 cure

30.1
1 load
2 exerted/imposed on
3 dynamic load
4 an impulse
5 static load
6 self-weight
7 magnitude
8 exerted/imposed on
9 loaded
10 uniformly distributed load
11 concentrated
12 point load

30.2
1 load-bearing
2 act, dead, live
3 magnitude, scalar
4 vector
5 stress, overstressed
6 strain
7 fails, failure

31.1

	↓					
1 →	S	A	G			
2 →	T	O	R	S	I	O	N
3 →	R	E	S	I	S	T
4 →	E	X	T	E	N	D
5 →	S	L	E	N	D	E	R
6 →	S	H	E	A	R

31.2   Mistake = '... the top of the beam is free from stress'. The top of the beam is in compression. The part of the beam which is free from stress is the neutral axis along the centreline of the beam.

31.3
1 bending
2 compression
3 neutral axis
4 tensile
5 fracturing
6 compressive
7 tension
8 crushing
9 deflect
10 sag
11 hog
12 deflection

32.1
1 statically determinate structures
2 counteracted
3 reaction
4 in equilibrium

32.2
1 component
2 resultant
3 pin joints
4 truss
5 centre of gravity

32.3   a = strut   b = strut   c = tie

32.4
1 frameworks
2 pin joint
3 compression
4 braced

33.1
1 linear
2 decelerate
3 rate
4 velocity
5 mass
6 inertia
7 accelerate
8 metres per second
9 metres per second squared
10 G-force

33.2
1 effort
2 pivots
3 turning moment / moment
4 simple machine
5 mechanical advantage
6 lever

34.1 1b, 2f, 3c, 4d, 5a, 6e

34.2
1 rotational
2 rotates / revolves
3 rotation / revolution
4 rotary / rotating / revolving
5 rotating / revolving
6 revolutions / revs
7 rotates / revolves

34.3
1 rev limit
2 rev limiter
3 rev counter
4 revved to
5 over-revved
6 high-revving

34.4
1 coefficient of friction
2 dynamic friction
3 static friction / stiction

35.1
1 chemical
2 kinetic
3 strain
4 useful
5 waste
6 light
7 sound
8 thermal

35.2
1 powered
2 source
3 gain
4 work
5 joules
6 power
7 wattage
8 powerful
9 efficiency
10 electrical
11 convert
12 form
13 chemical
14 stored
15 thermal
16 kinetic
17 efficient
18 useful
19 dissipated
20 waste

36.1
1 state, melts
2 boils/evaporates/vaporizes
3 cooled, solidifies
4 steam, water vapour
5 vapour
6 superheated steam

36.2 1b, 2a, 3e, 4c, 5d

36.3
2 exothermic
3 emitted
4 circulated
5 heat
6 heat
7 temperature
8 dissipated
9 convection
10 heat
11 absorbed
12 heating
13 conduction
14 condenses
15 latent

37.1
1 pipes
2 ducts
3 hose
4 pipe
5 water main
6 drain
7 sewer
8 fall

37.2 1a, 2a, 3b, 4a, 5b

37.3
1 A <u>turbine</u> is designed to be driven by a flow of air or gas.
2 A pump used to increase the pressure in a vessel is called a <u>compressor</u>.
3 A safety valve is an <u>outlet</u> which releases excess pressure.
4 A non-return valve is also called a <u>check</u> valve.
5 Some valves can be partly closed to <u>regulate</u> a flow, reducing its rate.

38.1
1 zero, negative
2 positive, negative
3 positive, zero
4 positive, positive

38.2
1 pressurized
2 at a lower pressure
3 atmospheric pressure
4 at a higher pressure
5 outside air
6 one atmosphere
7 gauge pressure
8 pressure differential
9 exert pressure on
10 explode
11 compressed air

38.3 1b, 2d, 3a, 4c

39.1
1 form drag, skin friction
2 downforce, lift
3 slipstream, wake
4 rotor, wing
5 CFD, wind tunnel

39.2
1 wake
2 lift
3 wind tunnel
4 skin friction
5 rotors

39.3
1 aerofoil
2 downforce
3 airflow
4 boundary layer
5 laminar flow
6 turbulent flow
7 drag
8 leading
9 trailing
10 pitch
11 downforce
12 drag
13 angle of attack

40.1
1 petrol
2 spark plug
3 mixture
4 piston cylinder
5 ignition
6 induction/intake
7 compression
8 fuel injector
9 power
10 torque

40.2
1 intake valve
2 combustion chamber
3 cylinder block
4 spark plug
5 exhaust valve
6 cylinder head
7 piston

41.1 An engine is connected to a driveshaft. Fitted to this <u>input</u> shaft is a gear wheel called the <u>driver</u>. As this gear wheel turns, it drives another gear wheel alongside it called a <u>follower</u>, which is fitted to an <u>output</u> shaft.

41.2
1 manual
2 shift
3 higher
4 automatic
5 selection
6 helical
7 wheels
8 ratio
9 shafts
10 transmit

41.3
1 Bevel/Crown/Worm
2 Helical
3 Worm
4 Idler

42.1
1 crank
2 bearings
3 sprocket
4 chain
5 sprocket

42.2
1 chain
2 sprocket
3 belt
4 pulley wheel
5 sprocket
6 chain
7 belt
8 pulley wheel
9 toothed

42.3
1 a cam
2 using a chain or a toothed belt
3 a follower
4 a flywheel
5 a piston and a crankshaft
6 a universal joint
7 a clutch
8 brake pads

43.1

1	ELECTRIC	C	U	R	R	E	N	T	
2	ELECTRIC	S	U	P	P	L	Y		
3	ELECTRIC	P	O	W	E	R			
4	ELECTRIC	C	O	N	D	U	C	T	O	R
5	ELECTRIC	I	N	S	U	L	A	T	O	R
6	ELECTRIC	C	H	A	R	G	E		
7	ELECTRIC	A	P	P	L	I	A	N	C	E
8	ELECTRIC	S	H	O	C	K			

43.2
1 current
2 circuit
3 amps
4 voltage
5 supply
6 volts
7 resistance
8 ohms
9 components
10 conductor
11 watts
12 wattage

44.1
1 direct current
2 alternating current
3 mains
4 frequency
5 hertz
6 sine wave
7 single-phase

44.2
a transmission
b field coils
c distribution
d grid
e step-up
f down

Order: 1b → 2e → 3a → 4f → 5c → 6d

44.3
1 true
2 true
3 false – Rechargeable batteries supply electricity as <u>direct</u> current.
4 false – Inverters convert <u>direct current</u> to alternating current.

45.1
1 power
2 series
3 integrated
4 short
5 parallel
6 printed

45.2
1 detector/sensor
2 detect/sense
3 logic gate
4 signal
5 switch on
6 switch off

45.3
a NOT gate

Index

The numbers in the index are Unit and Appendix numbers, not page numbers.

base metal /beɪs 'met.l/ 28
base plate /beɪs pleɪt/ 25
basement /'beɪs.mənt/ V
batch (v) /bætʃ/ 16
battery /'bæt.ri/ 43, XII
beam /biːm/ V
bear a load /beə rə ləʊd/ 30
bearing /'beə.rɪŋ/ XI
belt /belt/ 42
belt and braces
  /belt ən 'breɪ.sɪz/ 3
belt drive /belt draɪv/ 42
bend (v) /bend/ 31
bending /'ben.dɪŋ/ 31
bending stress
  /'ben.dɪŋ stres/ 31
bevel gear /'be.vəl ɡɪə/ 41
bhp (brake horsepower)
  /ˌbiː.jeɪtʃ'piː/ 40
billet /'bɪ.lɪt/ 21
bind /baɪnd/ 7
bit /bɪt/ 23
blade /bleɪd/
  as an aerofoil 39
  as part of
  a machine tool 23
blank /blæŋk/ 24
blanking /'blæŋ.kɪŋ/ 24
blind hole /blaɪnd həʊl/ 22
blind rivet /blaɪnd 'rɪ.vɪt/ 27
bloom (n) /bluːm/ 21
board /bɔːd/ 17, 21
boil /bɔɪl/ 2
boiler /'bɔɪ.lə/ 37
bolt /bəʊlt/ 26
bolt together /bəʊlt tə'ge.ðə/ 26
bolted joint /'bəʊl.tɪd dʒɔɪnt/ 26
bond (n) /bɒnd/ 29
bond (v) /bɒnd/ 29
bonding /'bɒn.dɪŋ/ 17
bore (n) /bɔː/ 6, X
bore (v) /bɔː/ 23
boundary layer
  /'baʊn.dri leɪ.ə/ 39
brace (n) /breɪs/ 32
brace (v) /breɪs/ 32
brake disc /breɪk dɪsk/ XI
brake horsepower (bhp)
  /breɪk 'hɔːs,paʊə/ 40
brake pad /breɪk pæd/ XI
brake (n) /breɪk/ XI
brass /brɑːs/ 13
brazed /breɪzd/ 29
brazing /'breɪ.zɪŋ/ 29

brick /brɪk/ 15
brittle /'brɪt.l/ 18
bronze /brɒnz/ 13
buckle (v) /'bʌk.l/ 31
buckling /'bʌk.lɪŋ/ 31
budget /'bʌdʒ.ɪt/ 3
bulb /bʌlb/ 43
bulk /bʌlk/ 21
c/c (centre-to-centre) /ˌsiː'siː/ 5
cable /'keɪ.bl/ 21, 42
CAD (computer aided
  design) /kæd/ 1
CAD/CAM (computer aided
  design/computer aided
  manufacturing)
  /'kæd,kæm/ 23
cam /kæm/ 42
camshaft /'kæm.ʃɑːft/ 42
cap /kæp/ IX
capacitor /kə'pæ.sɪ.tə/ XII
capacity /kə'pæ.sə.ti/ 10
carbon /'kɑː.bn/ 12, 15
carbon dioxide
  /'kɑː.bn daɪ'ɒk.saɪd/ 28
carbon steel /'kɑː.bn stiːl/ 12
carry a load /'kæ.ri jə ləʊd/ 30
case hardened
  /keɪs 'hɑː.dənd/ 20
case hardening
  /keɪs 'hɑː.dnɪŋ/ 20
cast (v) /kɑːst/
  as a process in forming
  concrete 16
  as a process in heating
  metal 20
cast in-situ (v)
  /kɑːst ɪn'sɪtjuː/ 16
casting /'kɑː.stɪŋ/ 20
cathode /'kæ.θəʊd/ 13
cavity /'kæv.ə.ti/ 22
cell /sel/ 43, XII
cement /sɪ'ment/ 16
cement-based /sɪ'ment beɪst/ 16
central /'sen.trəl/ 6
centre /'sen.tə/ 6
centre of gravity
  /'sen.tə rəv 'græv.ə.ti/ 32
centreline (CL) /'sen.tə,laɪn/ 5
centre-to-centre (c/c)
  /'sen.tə.tə'sen.tə/ 5
centrifugal clutch
  /ˌsen.trɪ'fjuː.ɡl klʌtʃ/ XI
centrifugal force
  /ˌsen.trɪ'fjuː.ɡl fɔːs/ 34

ceramic (adj) /sə'ræ.mɪk/ 15
ceramic (n) /sə'ræ.mɪk/ 15
CFD (computational fluid
  dynamics) /ˌsiː.jef'diː/ 39
chain /tʃeɪn/
  in polymers 14
  in transmission 42
chain dimensions
  /tʃeɪn ˌdaɪ'men.ʃənz/ 5
chain drive /'tʃeɪn draɪv/ 42
chamfered /'tʃæm.fəd/ 22
change /tʃeɪndʒ/ 41
channel /'tʃæn.l/ 22
charge /tʃɑːdʒ/ 44
charge carrier
  /tʃɑːdʒ 'kæ.riə/ 43
check valve /tʃek vælv/ IX
chemical anchor
  /'kem.ɪ.kl 'æŋ.kə/ 27
chemical bond
  /'kem.ɪ.kl bɒnd/ 29
chemical composition
  /'kem.ɪ.kl ˌkɒm.pə'zɪ.ʃən/ 11
chemical energy
  /'kem.ɪ.kl 'e.nə.dʒi/ 35
chemically bound
  /'kem.ɪ.kli baʊnd/ 11
chip (n) /tʃɪp/ 45
chipboard /'tʃɪp.bɔːd/ 17
chips /tʃɪps/ 23
chord /kɔːd/ 6
chromium /'krəʊ.mi.əm/ 12
CHS (circular hollow
  section) /ˌsiː.jeɪtʃ'es/ V
circle /'sɜː.kl/ 6
circuit /'sɜː.kɪt/ 43
circuit-breaker
  /'sɜː.kɪt 'breɪ.kə/ 45, XII
circular /'sɜː.kjə.lə/ 6
circular hollow section
  (CHS)
  /'sɜː.kjə.lə 'hɒ.ləʊ 'sek.ʃn/ V
circular saw
  /'sɜː.kjə.lə sɔː/ 17, 23
circulate /'sɜː.kjə.leɪt/ 36
circulate drawings
  /'sɜː.kjə.leɪt 'drɔː.ɪŋz/ 2
circumference /sə'kʌm.frəns/ 6
CL (centreline) /ˌsiː 'jəl/ 5
clamp load /klæmp ləʊd/ 26
clay /kleɪ/ 15
clearance /'klɪə.rəns/ 7
clearance fit /'klɪə.rəns fɪt/ 7
clockwise /'klɒk.waɪz/ 26

clockwise moment
/'klɒk.waɪz 'məʊ.mənt/ VI

close tolerance
/kləʊs 'tɒl.ə.rəns/ 7

clutch /klʌtʃ/ XI

coarse aggregate
/kɔːs 'æ.grɪ.gət/ 16

cobalt /'kəʊ.bɒlt/ 12

coefficient of friction
/ˌkəʊ.ɪ'fɪ.ʃənt əv 'frɪk.ʃən/ 34

coefficient of linear
expansion /ˌkəʊ.ɪ'fɪ.ʃənt əv
'lɪn.i.ə ɪk'spæn.ʃən/ 19

coefficient of thermal
expansion /ˌkəʊ.ɪ'fɪ.ʃənt əv
'θɜː.məl ɪk'spæn.ʃən/ 19

cog /kɒg/ 41

coil /kɔɪl/ 21

cold forged /kəʊld fɔːdʒd/ 20

cold rolled /kəʊld rəʊld/ 20

column /'kɒl.əm/ V

combustion /kəm'bʌs.tʃən/ 40

combustion chamber
/kəm'bʌs.tʃən 'tʃeɪm.bə/ 40

comment on a design
/'kɒ.ment ɒn ə dɪ'zaɪn/ 2

component /kəm'pəʊ.nənt/ 43

component force
/kəm'pəʊ.nənt fɔːs/ 32

composite (n) /'kɒm.pə.zɪt/ 11

composite material
/'kɒm.pə.zɪt mə'tɪə.ri.əl/ 11

compound /'kɒm.paʊnd/ 11

compound of
/'kɒm.paʊnd əv/ 11

compress (v) /kəm'pres/ 31

compressed air
/kəm'prest eə/ 37, 38

compressed gas
/kəm'prest gæs/ 38

compression /kəm'pre.ʃən/
as a form
of deformation 18, 31
in internal combustion
engines 40

compressive strength
/kəm'pre.sɪv strenθ/ 18

compressive stress
/kəm'pre.sɪv stres/ 31

compressor /kəm'pre.sə/ 37

computational fluid
dynamics (CFD)
/ˌkɒm.pjə'teɪ.ʃən.l
'fluː.ɪd daɪ'næ.mɪks/ 39

computer aided design (CAD)
/kəm'pjuː.tə 'eɪ.dɪd dɪ'zaɪn/ 1

computer aided design/
computer aided
manufacturing (CAD/
CAM) /kəm'pjuː.tə.ə'eɪ.dɪd
dɪ'zaɪn/, /kəm'pjuː.tə.ə'eɪ.dɪd
ˌmæn.jə'fæk.tʃrɪŋ/ 23

computer numerical
control (CNC) /kəm'pjuː.tə
njuː'mer.ɪ.kl kən'trəʊl/ 23

concentrate (v)
/'kɒn.sən.treɪt/ 30

concentrated /'kɒnt.sən.treɪ.tɪd/ V

concentric circles
/kən'sen.trɪk 'sɜː.klz/ 6

concept /'kɒn.sept/ 2

concrete /'kɒŋ.kriːt/ 16

condense /kən'dens/ 36

conduct (v) /kən'dʌkt/
as a process in heat
transfer 19, 36
as a process of an electric
current 43

conduction /kən'dʌk.ʃən/ 36

conductor /kən'dʌk.tə/ 43

conical spring washer
/'kɒn.ɪ.kl sprɪŋ 'wɒ.ʃə/ 26

connect to /kə'nekt tə/ 25

connect together
/kə'nekt tə'ge.ðə/ 25

connecting rod (conrod)
/kə'nek.tɪŋ rɒd/ 42

connection /kə'nek.ʃən/ 25

conrod (connecting rod)
/'kɒn.rɒd/ 42

constant /'kɒn.stənt/ 10

constant radius
/'kɒn.stənt 'reɪ.di.əs/ 6

constituent /kən'stɪt.ju.ənt/ 11

constraint /kən'streɪnt/ 3

consumable /kən'sjuː.mə.bl/ 28

consume /kən'sjuːm/
as a process in supply,
demand and capacity 10
as a process in welding 28

consumption /kən'sʌm.ʃən/ 10

contact adhesive
/'kɒn.tækt əd'hiː.sɪv/ 29

contract (v) /kən'trækt/ 7, 19

contraction /kən'træk.ʃn/ 7, 19

control system
/kən'trəʊl 'sɪs.təm/ 45

convection /kən'vek.ʃən/ 36

convector /kən'vek.tə/ 36

convert (v) /kən'vɜːt/ 34, 35

cool (v) /kuːl/ 36

coolant /'kuː.lənt/
in machining 23
in radiators VII

cooling systems
/'kuː.lɪŋ 'sɪ.stəmz/ VII

coordinate dimensions
/kəʊ'ɔː.dɪ.nət ˌdaɪ'men.ʃənz/ 5

copper /'kɒ.pə/ 13

core /kɔː/ 23

core drilling /kɔː 'drɪ.lɪŋ/ 23

corrode /kə'rəʊd/ 12

corrosion /kə'rəʊ.ʒən/ 12

cost-effective /ˌkɒst.ɪ'fek.tɪv/ 3

counteract /ˌkaʊn.tər'ækt/ 32

countersinking
/'kaʊn.tə.sɪŋ.kɪŋ/ 22

countersunk /'kaʊn.tə.sʌŋk/ 22

couple /kʌp.l/ 40

crank /kræŋk/ 42

crankshaft /'kræŋk.ʃɑːft/ 42

creep /kriːp/ 19

cross (n) /krɒs/ IX

crosshead screw
/'krɒs,hed skruː/ 27

cross-member
/krɒs 'mem.bə/ 32

cross-section /'krɒs.sek.ʃn/ 1

cross-sectional area
/krɒs 'sek.ʃən.l 'eə.ri.ə/ 9

crown /kraʊn/ 6

crown gear /kraʊn gɪə/ 41

crush /krʌʃ/ 31

crushing /'krʌʃ.ɪŋ/ 31

cubic metre (m³)
/'kjuː.bɪk 'miː.tə/ 9

cumulative /'kjuː.mjə.lə.tɪv/ 10

cure (v) /kjʊə/
as a process of
polymers 14
as a process of
adhesives 29

current (n) /'kʌ.rənt/ 43

current drawing
/'kʌ.rənt 'drɔː.ɪŋ/ 2

curve (n) /kɜːv/ 6

curved /kɜːvd/ 6

cutting fluid /'kʌ.tɪŋ 'fluː.ɪd/ 23

cycle /'saɪ.kl/ 40

cyclic loads /'saɪ.klɪk ləʊdz/ 19

cylinder /'sɪ.lɪn.də/ 40

cylinder block /ˈsɪ.lɪn.də blɒk/ 40

cylinder head /ˈsɪ.lɪn.də hed/ 40

dam /dæm/ V

DC (direct current) /ˌdiːˈsiː/ 44

DC supply /ˌdiːˈsiː səˈplaɪ/ 44

dead load /ded ləʊd/ V

decelerate /diːˈsel.ə.reɪt/ 33

deceleration /ˌdiːˌsel.əˈreɪ.ʃən/ 33

decimal number /ˈde.sɪ.məl ˈnʌm.bə/ 8

deflect /dɪˈflekt/ 31

deflection /dɪˈflek.ʃən/ 31

deform /dɪˈfɔːm/ 6, 18, 27, 30

deformation /ˌdiː.fəˈmeɪ.ʃən/ 6, 18

deformed /dɪˈfɔːmd/ 6

degrees Celsius (°C) /dɪˈɡriːz ˈsel.si.əs/ 36

demand (n) /dɪˈmɑːnd/ 10

dense /dens/ 9

density /ˈden.sɪ.ti/ 9

design brief /dɪˈzaɪn briːf/ 2

design concept /dɪˈzaɪn ˈkɒn.sept/ 2

design solution /dɪˈzaɪn səˈluː.ʃən/ 3

designed to do /dɪˈzaɪnd tə duː/ 3

detail (n) /ˈdiː.teɪl/ 1

detail drawing /ˈdiː.teɪl ˈdrɔː.ɪŋ/ 1

detect /dɪˈtekt/ 45

detector /dɪˈtek.tə/ 45

determine /dɪˈtɜː.mɪn/ 3

deviate /ˈdiː.vi.eɪt/ 7

deviation /ˌdiː.viˈeɪ.ʃən/ 7

diagonal (n) /daɪˈæɡ.ən.l/ 5

diagonal measurement /daɪˈæɡ.ən.l ˈme.ʒə.mənt/ 5

diameter /daɪˈæm.ɪt.ə/ 6

diamond /ˈdaɪə.mənd/ 15

diamond drilling /ˈdaɪə.mənd ˈdrɪ.lɪŋ/ 23

die (n) /daɪ/ 20, 24

diesel engine /ˈdiː.zl ˈen.dʒɪn/ 40

dim (dimension) /dɪm/ 4

dimension (dim) /ˌdaɪˈmen.ʃən/ 4

diode /ˈdaɪ.əʊd/ XII

direct current (DC) /dɪˈrekt ˈkʌ.rənt/ 44

direct the flow /dɪˈrekt ðə fləʊ/ IX

disc brake /dɪsk breɪk/ XI

discontinuity /ˌdɪsˌkɒn.tɪˈnjuː.ə.ti/ 28

disproportional /ˌdɪs.prəˈpɔː.ʃən.l/ 30

dissimilar materials /ˌdɪsˈsɪm.ɪ.lə məˈtɪə.ri.əlz/ 28

dissipate /ˈdɪs.ɪ.peɪt/ 35, 36

distribution line /ˌdɪs.trɪˈbjuː.ʃn laɪn/ 44

divide by /dɪˈvaɪd baɪ/ 8

double-check /ˌdʌb.lˈtʃek/ 5

downforce /ˈdaʊn.fɔːs/ 39

downstream of /ˌdaʊnˈstriːm əv/ 39

draft version /drɑːft ˈvɜː.ʃən/ 2

drag /dræɡ/ 39

drag coefficient /dræɡ ˌkəʊ.ɪˈfɪ.ʃənt/ 39

drain /dreɪn/ 37

drawing (dwg) /ˈdrɔː.ɪŋ/ 1

drawn to scale /drɔːn tə skeɪl/ 1

drill (n) /drɪl/ 23

drill bit /drɪl bɪt/ 23

drill into /drɪl ˈɪn.tə/ 23

drilling /ˈdrɪ.lɪŋ/ 23

drive (n) /draɪv/ 41

drive (v) /draɪv/ 40, 41

driver /ˈdraɪ.və/ 41

driveshaft /ˈdraɪvˌʃɑːft/ 41

drop forging /drɒp ˈfɔː.dʒɪŋ/ 20

drop-forged /drɒp fɔːdʒ.d/ 20

drum brake /drʌm breɪk/ XI

drum /drʌm/ XI

duct /dʌkt/ 37

ductile /ˈdʌk.taɪl/ 18

ductwork /dʌkt.wɜːk/ 37

durability /ˌdjʊə.rəˈbɪ.lə.ti/ 19

durable /ˈdjʊə.rə.bl/ 19

dwg (drawing) /ˈdrɔː.ɪŋ/ 1

dynamic friction /daɪˈnæ.mɪk ˈfrɪk.ʃən/ 34

dynamic load /daɪˈnæ.mɪk ləʊd/ 30, V

earth (v) /ɜːθ/ 45

earthed /ɜːθ.t/ 45

edge quality /edʒ ˈkwɒ.lə.ti/ 24

EDM (electrical discharge machining) /ˌiː.diːˈjem/ 24

efficiency /ɪˈfɪ.ʃən.si/ 10, 35

efficiency gain /ɪˈfɪ.ʃən.si ɡeɪn/ 35

efficient /ɪˈfɪ.ʃənt/ 10, 35

effort /ˈe.fət/ 33

elastic (adj) /ɪˈlæs.tɪk/ 18

elastic deformation /ɪˈlæs.tɪk ˌdiː.fəˈmeɪ.ʃən/ 18

elastic limit /ɪˈlæs.tɪk ˈlɪ.mɪt/ 18

elastically deformed /ɪˈlæs.tɪk.li dɪˈfɔːmd/ 18

elasticity /ˌɪl.æsˈtɪs.ə.ti/ 18

elastomer /ɪˈlæs.tɪm.ə/ 14

electric arc /ɪˈlek.trɪk ɑːk/ 24

electric charge /ɪˈlek.trɪk tʃɑːdʒ/ 43

electric circuit /ɪˈlek.trɪk ˈsɜː.kɪt/ 43

electric current /ɪˈlek.trɪk ˈkʌ.rənt/ 43

electric motor /ɪˈlek.trɪk ˈməʊ.tə/ 40

electric shock /ɪˈlek.trɪk ʃɒk/ 43

electrical /ɪˈlek.trɪ.kl/ 45

electrical appliance /ɪˈlek.trɪ.kl əˈplaɪ.əns/ 43

electrical cable /ɪˈlek.trɪ.kl ˈkeɪ.bl/ 21

electrical component /ɪˈlek.trɪ.kl kəmˈpəʊ.nənt/ 43

electrical conductor /ɪˈlek.trɪ.kl kənˈdʌk.tə/ 43

electrical discharge machining (EDM) /ɪˈlek.trɪ.kl ˈdɪs.tʃɑːdʒ məˈʃiː.nɪŋ/ 24

electrical energy /ɪˈlek.trɪ.kl ˈen.ə.dʒi/ 35

electrical insulator /ɪˈlek.trɪ.kl ˈɪn.sjə.leɪ.tə/ 43

electrical power /ɪˈlek.trɪ.kl paʊə/ 43

electrical resistance /ɪˈlek.trɪ.kl rɪˈzɪs.təns/ 43

electrical supply /ɪˈlek.trɪ.kl ˈsə.plaɪ/ 43

electrical wire /ɪˈlek.trɪ.kl waɪə/ 21

electrode /ɪˈlek.trəʊd/ 28

electro-galvanized /ɪˈlek.trəʊ ˈɡæl.və.naɪzd/ 13

electrolyte /ɪˈlek.trə.laɪt/ 13

electromagnetic induction /ɪˌlek.trə.mæɡˈnet.ɪk ɪnˈdʌk.ʃən/ 44

electromagnetic waves /ɪˌlek.trə.mæɡˈnet.ɪk weɪvz/ 36

electromotive force (EMF) /ɪˌlek.trəˈməʊ.tɪv fɔːs/ 43

electron /ɪˈlek.trɒn/ 22, 43

electronic /ˌe.lekˈtrɒ.nɪk/ 45

electroplating /ɪˈlek.trəʊ.pleɪ.tɪŋ/ 13

element /ˈe.lɪ.mənt/ 11

elevation /ˌel.ɪˈveɪ.ʃən/ 1

elongation /ˌiː.lɒŋˈgeɪ.ʃən/ 18
embed in /ɪmˈbed ɪn/ 25
EMF (electromotive force)
/ˌiː.jemˈef/ 43
emit /ɪˈmɪt/ 36
endothermic /en.dəˈθɜː.mɪk/ 36
energy /ˈen.ə.dʒi/ 35
energy source /ˈen.ə.dʒi sɔːs/ 35
engine /ˈen.dʒɪn/ 40
engineered wood
/ˌen.dʒɪˈnɪ.əd wʊd/ 17
engineering plastic
/ˌen.dʒɪˈnɪ.ə.ɪŋ ˈplæs.tɪk/ 14
enlarge /ɪnˈlɑːdʒ/ 23
enlarged /ɪnˈlɑːdʒ.d/ 1
epoxy resin
/ɪˈpɒk.si ˈre.zɪn/ 14, 29
equal (adj) /ˈiː.kwəl/ 8
equal (v) /ˈiː.kwəl/ 8
equal to (adj) /ˈiː.kwəl tə/ 8
evaluate /ɪˈvæl.ju.eɪt/ 3
evaporate /ɪˈvæp.ə.reɪt/ 29, 36
evaporation /ɪˌvæp.əˈreɪ.ʃən/ 36
exceed /ɪkˈsiːd/ 3, 10
exert force on
/ɪgˈzɜːt fɔːs ɒn/ 30
exert pressure on
/ɪgˈzɜːt ˈpre.ʃə rɒn/ 38
exhaust /ɪgˈzɔːst/ 40
exhaust gases
/ɪgˈzɔːst ˈgæ.sɪz/ 40
exhaust valve /ɪgˈzɔːst vælv/ 40
existing model
/ɪgˈzɪs.tɪŋ ˈmɒd.l/ 3
exothermic /ek.səˈθɜː.mɪk/ 36
expand /ɪkˈspænd/ 7, 19, 27
expansion /ɪkˈspæn.ʃən/ 7, 19
expansion anchor
/ɪkˈspæn.ʃən ˈæŋ.kə/ 27
explode /ɪkˈspləʊd/ 38
exploded view
/ɪkˈspləʊd.ɪd vjuː/ 1, I
extend /ɪkˈstend/ 30, 31
extension /ɪkˈsten.ʃən/ 18, 30
external /ɪkˈstɜː.nəl/ 4
external force
/ɪkˈstɜː.nəl fɔːs/ 33
extremity /ɪkˈstrem.ə.ti/ 4
extruding /ɪkˈstruː.dɪŋ/ 20
extrusion /ɪkˈstruː.ʒən/ 20
face (n) /feɪs/ 4
factor in /ˈfæk.tə rɪn/ 3
factor of safety
/ˈfæk.tə rɒv ˈseɪf.ti/ 3

factory head /ˈfæk.tri hed/ 27
fail /feɪl/ 30
failure /ˈfeɪl.jə/ 30
fall (n) /fɔːl/ 37
fan /fæn/ 37
fasten to /ˈfɑː.sn tə/ 25
fasten together
/ˈfɑː.sn təˈge.ðə/ 25
fastener /ˈfɑːs.nə/ 26
fatigue /fəˈtiːg/ 19
fatigue cracking
/fəˈtiːg ˈkræ.kɪŋ/ 19
feature /ˈfiː.tʃə/ 3
ferrous metal /ˈfe.rəs ˈmet.l/ 11
fibres /ˈfaɪ.bəz/ 21
field coil /ˈfiːld kɔɪl/ 44
field winding /ˈfiːld ˈwaɪn.dɪŋ/ 44
filament /ˈfɪl.ə.mənt/ 43
fill /fɪl/ 25
filler /ˈfɪl.ə/ 28
fine aggregate /faɪn ˈæ.grɪ.gət/ 16
fire (v) /faɪə/ 15
fit (n) /fɪt/ 7
fit together /fɪt təˈge.ðə/ 25
fit together /fɪt təˈge.ðə/ 7
fix to /fɪks tə/ 25
fix together /fɪks təˈge.ðə/ 25
fixing /ˈfɪk.sɪŋ/ 26
flame-cutting /fleɪm ˈkʌt.ɪŋ/ 24
flange /flændʒ/ IX
flat /flæt/ 4
flat bar /flæt bɑː/ 21
flat head /flæt hed/ 22
flat washer /flæt ˈwɒʃ.ə/ 26
flex (v) /fleks/ 31, 19
flexure /ˈflek.ʃə/ 31
float glass /fləʊt glɑːs/ 15
flow (n) /fləʊ/ 37
flow (v) /fləʊ/ 43, 37
flow rate /fləʊ reɪt/ IX
flowmeter /fləʊ ˈmiː.tə/ XIII
fluctuate /ˈflʌk.tʃu.eɪt/ 10
fluctuation /ˌflʌk.tʃuˈeɪ.ʃən/ 10
fluid /ˈfluː.ɪd/ 38
fluid dynamics
/ˈfluː.ɪd daɪˈnæ.mɪks/ 39
flush /flʌʃ/ 22
flush with /flʌʃ wɪð/ 22
flux /flʌks/ 28
flywheel /ˈflaɪ.wiːl/ 42
follower /ˈfɒl.əʊ.ə/ 41, 42
forge (n) /fɔːdʒ/ 20
forged /fɔːdʒ.d/ 20
forging /ˈfɔːdʒ.ɪŋ/ 20

form (v) /fɔːm/ 20
form drag /fɔːm dræg/ 39
form of energy
/fɔːm əv ˈen.ə.dʒi/ 35
formwork /fɔːm.wɜːk/ 16
forty-five-degree elbow
/ˈfɔːti faɪv dɪˈgriː ˈel.bəʊ/ IX
foundation /faʊnˈdeɪ.ʃn/ V
four atmospheres
/fɔː ˈæt.məs.fɪəz/ 38
four bar /fɔː bɑː/ 38
four-stroke engine
/fɔː strəʊk ˈen.dʒɪn/ 40
fraction /ˈfræk.ʃn/ 8
fracture (v) /ˈfræk.tʃə/ 18, 31
fracture point
/ˈfræk.tʃə pɔɪnt/ 18
fracture toughness
/ˈfræk.tʃə ˈtʌf.nəs/ 19
frame /freɪm/ 32
framework /ˈfreɪm.wɜːk/ 32
free fall /friː fɔːl/ 33
frequency /ˈfriː.kwənt.si/ 44
friction /ˈfrɪk.ʃən/ 34
frictional resistance
/ˈfrɪk.ʃən.l rɪˈzɪs.təns/ 34
fuel injector
/ˈfjuː.əl ɪnˈdʒek.tə/ 40
fuel line /ˈfjuː.əl laɪn/ 37
fulcrum /ˈfʊl.krəm/ 33
function /ˈfʌŋ.ʃən/ 3
fuse (v) /fjuːz/ 28
fuse (n) /fjuːz/ XII
fusion /ˈfjuː.ʒən/ 28
fusion zone /ˈfjuː.ʒən zəʊn/ 28
GA (general arrangement)
/ˌdʒiː ˈeɪ/ 1
gain /geɪn/ 10
galvanizing /ˈgæl.və.naɪ.zɪŋ/ 13
gamma rays /ˈgæm.ə reɪz/ VII
gap /gæp/ 25
gas bottle /gæs ˈbɒt.l/ 37
gas cylinder /gæs ˈsɪl.ɪn.də/ 37
gas main /gæs meɪn/ 37
gas metal arc welding
(GMAW)
/gæs ˈmet.l ɑːk ˈwel.dɪŋ/ 28
gas tungsten arc welding
(GTAW)
/gæs ˈtʌŋ.stən ɑːk ˈwel.dɪŋ/ 28
gas welding /gæs ˈwel.dɪŋ/ 28
gauge pressure /geɪdʒ ˈpre.ʃə/ 38
gear /gɪə/ 41
gear ratio /gɪə ˈreɪ.ʃi.əʊ/ 41

gear selection /gɪə sɪˈlek.ʃən/ 41
gear train /gɪə treɪn/ 41
gear wheel /gɪə wiːl/ 41
gearbox /ˈgɪə.bɒks/ 41
general arrangement (GA)
　/ˈdʒen.rəl əˈreɪndʒ.mənt/ 1
generate /ˈdʒen.ə.reɪt/ 44
generator /ˈdʒen.ə.reɪ.tə/ 44
G-force /ˈdʒiː ˌfɔːs/ 33
glass-like /glɑːs laɪk/ 15
glass-reinforced plastic (GRP)
　/glɑːs ˌriː.ɪnˈfɔːst ˈplæs.tɪk/ 11
glue (n) /gluː/ 29
glue together /gluː təˈge.ðə/ 29
glue-laminated (glulams)
　/gluː ˈlæm.ɪn.eɪ.tɪd/ 17
glulams (glue-laminated)
　/ˈgluːˌlæmz/ 17
go back to the drawing board
　/gəʊ bæk tə ðə ˈdrɔː.ɪŋ bɔːd/ 2
go rusty /gəʊ ˈrʌs.ti/ 12
gold /gəʊld/ 13
grade (n) /greɪd/ 12
grain /greɪn/ 17
gram (g) /græm/ 9
gravity /ˈgræv.ə.ti/ 9, 32
grease /griːs/ XI
grid /grɪd/ 5, 44
　in electrical supply 5
　in drawing 44
gridline /ˈgrɪd.laɪn/ 5
grind (v) /graɪnd/ 23
grinder /ˈgraɪn.də/ 23
grinding /ˈgraɪn.dɪŋ/ 23
groove /gruːv/ 22
ground beam /graʊnd biːm/ V
ground level /graʊnd ˈlev.l/ V
ground/grounded
　/graʊnd/, /ˈgraʊn.dɪd/ 45
GRP (glass-reinforced
　plastic) /ˌdʒiː.jaːˈpiː/ 11
grub screw /grʌb skruː/ 27
guillotine (n) /ˈgɪl.ə.tiːn/ 24
guillotine (v) /ˈgɪl.ə.tiːn/ 24
hacksaw /ˈhæk.sɔː/ 23
hard /hɑːd/ 19
hard soldering
　/hɑːd ˈsəʊl.drɪŋ/ 29
hardness /ˈhɑːd.nəs/ 19
hardwood /ˈhɑːd.wʊd/ 17
have the potential
　/hæv ðə pəˈten.ʃəl/ 35
HAZ (heat-affected zone)
　/ˌeɪtʃ.eɪˈzed/ 24, 28
head /hed/ 26

head of water /hed əv ˈwɔː.tə/ 38
header tank /ˈhed.ə tæŋk/ 38
heat (n) /hiːt/ 36
heat (v) /hiːt/ 36
heat exchanger
　/hiːt ɪksˈtʃeɪn.dʒə/ 36
heat sink /hiːt sɪŋk/ VII
heat source /hiːt sɔːs/ 36
heat transfer /hiːt ˈtræns.fɜː/ 36
heat treating /hiːt ˈtriː.tɪŋ/ 20
heat treatment
　/hiːt ˈtriːt.mənt/ 20
heat-affected zone (HAZ)
　/hiːt əˈfek.tɪd zəʊn/ 24, 28
heating system
　/ˈhiːt.ɪŋ ˈsɪs.təm/ 36
height /haɪt/ 4
helical /ˈhiː.lɪ.kl/ 26
helical gear /ˈhiː.lɪ.kl gɪə/ 41
helical spring washer
　/ˈhiː.lɪ.kl sprɪŋ ˈwɒ.ʃə/ 26
Hertz (Hz) /hɜːts/ 44
hex head /heks hed/ 26
hex key /heks kiː/ 26
hexagonal head
　/hekˈsæg.ən.l hed/ 26
high carbon steel
　/haɪ ˈkɑː.bn stiːl/ 12
high revs /haɪ revz/ 34
high strength friction grip
　(HSFG)
　/haɪ streŋθ ˈfrɪk.ʃən grip/ 26
high strength low alloy steel
　(HSLA)
　/haɪ streŋθ ləʊ ˈæ.lɔɪ stiːl/ 12
higher gear /ˈhaɪ.ə gɪə/ 41
high-revving /haɪ ˈrev.ɪŋ/ 34
high-speed steel
　/haɪ spiːd stiːl/ 12
high-voltage (HV)
　/haɪ ˈvəʊl.tɪdʒ/ 44
hog /hɒg/ 31
hold together
　/həʊld təˈge.ðə/ 25
holesaw /ˈhəʊl.sɔː/ 23
hollow /ˈhɒ.ləʊ/ 21
horizontal plane
　/ˌhɒ.rɪˈzɒn.tl pleɪn/ 4
horsepower (hp) /ˈhɔːsˌpaʊə/ 40
hose /həʊz/ 37
hose coupling /həʊz ˈkʌp.lɪŋ/ 37
hose fitting /həʊz ˈfɪt.ɪŋ/ 37
hot forged /hɒt fɔːdʒd/ 20
hot rolled /hɒt rəʊld/ 20

hot-dip galvanized
　/hɒt dɪp ˈgæl.və.naɪzd/ 13
hp (horsepower) /ˌeɪtʃˈpiː/ 40
HSFG (high strength friction
　grip) /ˌeɪtʃˈes.ef.dʒiː/ 26
HV (high-voltage) /ˌeɪtʃˈviː/ 44
hydrostatic pressure
　/ˌhaɪ.drəˈstæt.ɪk ˈpre.ʃə/ 38
hygrometer /haɪˈgrɒm.ɪ.tə/ XIII
ID (inside diameter) /ˌaɪˈdiː/ 6
idler /ˈaɪd.lə/ 41
idler gear /ˈaɪd.lə gɪə/ 41
ignite /ɪgˈnaɪt/ 40
ignition /ɪgˈnɪʃ.n/ 40
immerse /ɪˈmɜːs/ X
imperial /ɪmˈpɪə.riəl/ 8
implode /ɪmˈpləʊd/ 38
imposed on /ɪmˈpəʊzd ɒn/ 30, V
imprecise /ˌɪm.prɪˈsaɪs/ 7
impulse /ˈɪm.pʌls/ 30, V
in bending /ɪn ˈben.dɪŋ/ 31
in compression
　/ɪn kəmˈpreʃ.n/ 31
in equilibrium
　/ɪn ˌiː.kwɪˈlɪb.riəm/ 32
in motion /ɪn ˈməʊ.ʃn/ 33
in shear /ɪn ʃɪə/ 31
in tension /ɪn ˈten.ʃən/ 18, 31
in torsion /ɪn ˈtɔː.ʃən/ 31
inaccurate /ɪnˈæk.jə.rət/ 7
inclined /ɪnˈklaɪnd/ 4
inclined from /ɪnˈklaɪnd frəm/ 4
indentation /ˌɪn.denˈteɪ.ʃən/ 19
indentation hardness
　/ˌɪn.denˈteɪ.ʃən ˈhɑːd.nəs/ 19
induction /ɪnˈdʌk.ʃən/ 40
inductor /ɪnˈdʌk.tə/ XII
industrial diamond
　/ɪnˈdʌs.tri.əl ˈdaɪə.mənd/ 15
inefficient /ˌɪn.ɪˈfɪ.ʃənt/ 10
inertia /ɪˈnɜː.ʃə/ 33
infrared /ˌɪn.frəˈred/ VII
ingot /ˈɪŋ.gət/ 21
inlet /ˈɪn.let/ IX
inner circle /ˈɪn.ə ˈsɜː.kl/ 6
inorganic /ˌɪn.ɔːˈgæn.ɪk/ 15
input /ˈɪn.pʊt/ 10
input shaft /ˈɪn.pʊt ʃɑːft/ 41
input speed /ˈɪn.pʊt spiːd/ 41
inside diameter (ID) /ˌɪnˈsaɪd
　daɪˈæ.mɪt.ə/ 6
in-situ concrete
　/ɪnˈsit.juː ˈkɒŋ.kriːt/ 16
insufficient clearance
　/ˌɪn.səˈfɪ.ʃənt ˈklɪə.rəns/ 7

insulate /'ɪn.sjə.leɪt/ 43
insulation /ˌɪn.sjə'leɪ.ʃən/ 43
insulator /'ɪn.sjə.leɪ.tə/ 43
intake /'ɪn.teɪk/ 40
intake valve /'ɪn.teɪk vælv/ 40
integrated circuit
  /'ɪn.tɪ.greɪt.ɪd 'sɜː.kɪt/ 45
interference drag
  /ˌɪn.tə'fɪə.rəns dræg/ 39
interference fit
  /ˌɪn.tə'fɪə.rəns fɪt/ 7
interlock /ˌɪn.tə'lɒk/ 41
internal /ɪn'tɜː.nəl/ 4
internal combustion engine
  /ɪn'tɜː.nəl kəm'bʌs.tʃən 'en.dʒɪn/
  40
intersect at /ˌɪn.tə'sekt ət/ 5
invert (n) /'ɪn.vɜːt/ 6
inverter /ɪn'vɜː.tə/ 44, XII
ionize (v) /'aɪə.naɪz/ 24
iron /aɪən/ 12
iron ore /aɪən ɔː/ 15
iron oxide /aɪən 'ɒk.saɪd/ 12
iron–carbon alloy
  /ˌaɪən'kɑː.bn 'æ.lɔɪ/ 11
I-section /aɪ 'sek.ʃn/ 21
isolate (v) /'aɪs.ə.leɪt/ 45
isometric projection
  /ˌaɪs.ə'met.rɪk prə'dʒek.ʃn/ 1, I
issue drawings /'ɪ.ʃuː drɔː.ɪŋz/ 2
J (joule) /dʒeɪ/ 35
jet /dʒet/ 40
jet engine /dʒet 'en.dʒɪn/ 40
join to /dʒɔɪn tə/ 25
join together /dʒɔɪn tə'ge.ðə/ 25
joint /dʒɔɪnt/ 25
joule (J) /dʒuːl/ 35
kerf /kɜːf/ 23
kg (kilogram) /'kɪl.ə.græm/ 9
kg/m³ (kilograms per cubic
  metre)
  /'kɪl.ə.græmz pə 'kjuː.bɪk miː.tə/ 9
kilogram (kg) /'kɪl.ə.græm/ 9
kilograms per cubic metre
  (kg/m³)
  /'kɪl.ə.græmz pə 'kjuː.bɪk miː.tə/ 9
kinetic energy
  /kɪ'net.ɪk 'en.ə.dʒi/ 35
knot /nɒt/ 17
laminar /'læm.ɪn.ə/ 39
laminar flow /'læm.ɪn.ə fləʊ/ 39
laminate with
  /'læm.ɪ.neɪt wɪð/ 15
laminated /'læm.ɪ.neɪt.ɪd/ 15

laminated glass
  /'læm.ɪ.neɪ.tɪd glɑːs/ 15
lamp /læmp/ 43, XII
large scale /lɑːdʒ skeɪl/ 1
large-section /lɑːdʒ 'sek.ʃn/ 9
laser beam /'leɪ.zə biːm/ 22
laser cutting /'leɪ.zə 'kʌt.ɪŋ/ 24
latent heat /'leɪ.tənt hiːt/ 36
latent heat of fusion
  /'leɪ.tənt hiːt əv 'fjuː.ʒən/ 36
latent heat of vaporization
  /'leɪ.tənt hiːt əv
  ˌveɪ.pə.raɪ'zeɪ.ʃən/ 36
latex /'leɪ.teks/ 14
lathe /leɪð/ 23
lattice /'læ.tɪs/ 32
layer /leɪə/ 15
lead /led/ 13
leading edge /'liː.d.ɪŋ edʒ/ 39
left-hand thread
  /'left.hænd θred/ 26
length /leŋθ/ 4
less /les/ 8
less powerful /les 'paʊə.fəl/ 35
level /lev.l/ 4
lever /'liː.və/, /'le.və/ 33
leverage /'liː.və.rɪdʒ/,
  /'le.və.rɪdʒ/ 33
lift /lɪft/ 39
light energy /laɪt 'en.ə.dʒi/ 35
lightweight /'laɪt.weɪt/ 9
limit of proportionality
  /'lɪm.ɪt
  əv prə.pɔː.ʃən'æl.ə.ti/ 18, 30
linear /'lɪn.iə/ 33
linear acceleration /'lɪn.iə
  ək.sel.ə'reɪ.ʃən/ 33
linear motion /'lɪn.iə 'məʊ.ʃn/
  33
live (adj) /laɪv/ 43, 45
live load /laɪv ləʊd/ 30, V
load /ləʊd/ 3, 30, 33
load-bearing /ləʊd 'beə.rɪŋ/ 30
loaded /'ləʊd.ɪd/ 30
locate /ləʊ'keɪt/ 5
logic gate /'lɒdʒ.ɪk geɪt/ 45
loose tolerance
  /luːs 'tɒl.ə.rəns/ 7
loosen /'luː.sən/ 26
loss /lɒs/ 10
low alloy steel
  /ləʊ 'æ.lɔɪ stiːl/ 12
low revs /ləʊ revz/ 34
lower gear /'ləʊ.ə gɪə/ 41

low-voltage (LV)
  /ləʊ 'vəʊl.tɪdʒ/ 44
lubricant /'luː.brɪ.kənt/ XI
lumber /'lʌm.bə/ 17
LV (low-voltage) /ˌel'viː/ 44
m/s (metres per second)
  /'miː.təz pə 'sek.ənd/ 33
m/s² (metres per second
  squared)
  /'miː.təz pə 'sek.ənd skweəd/ 33
m³ (cubic metre)
  /kjuː.bɪk 'miː.tə/ 9
machine (v) /mə'ʃiːn/ 23
machine (n) /mə'ʃiːn/ 33
machine screw
  /mə'ʃiːn skruː/ 27
machine tools /mə'ʃiːn tuːlz/ 23
machining /mə'ʃiːn.ɪŋ/ 23
magnesium /mæg'niː.zi.əm/ 13
magnitude /'mæg.nɪ.tjuːd/ 30
mains /meɪnz/ 37
mains electricity
  /meɪnz ɪˌlek'trɪ.sɪ.ti/ 44
malleable /'mæl.i.ə.bl/ 18
manganese /'mæŋ.gə.niːz/ 12
manmade /ˌmæn'meɪd/ 14
manual gearbox /'mæn.ju.əl
  'gɪə.bɒks/ 41
mass /mæs/ 9, 33
materials testing machine
  /mə'tɪə.ri.əlz tes.tɪŋ mə'ʃiːn/ 30
matrix /'meɪ.trɪks/ 11
MDF (medium-density
  fibreboard) /ˌem.diː'jef/ 17
measure along /'meʒ.ə rə'lɒŋ/ 4
measure from/to (v) /
  'meʒ.ə frəm/, /'meʒ.ə tə/ 4
measure vertically/
  horizontally /'meʒ.ə 'vɜː.tɪk.li/,
  /'meʒ.ə ˌhɒ.rɪ'zɒn.tə.li/ 4
mechanical advantage
  /mɪ'kæn.ɪ.kl əd'vɑːn.tɪdʒ/ 33
mechanical bond
  /mɪ'kæn.ɪ.kl bɒnd/ 29
mechanical energy
  /mɪ'kæn.ɪ.kl 'en.ə.dʒi/ 35
mechanically stress-graded
  /mɪ'kæn.ɪ.kli stres 'greɪd.ɪd/ 17
medium carbon steel
  /'miː.di.əm 'kɑː.bn stiːl/ 12
medium-density fibreboard
  (MDF) /'miː.di.əm 'den.sɪ.ti
  ˌfaɪ.bə'bɔːd/ 17
meet demand /miːt dɪ'mɑːnd/ 10

perfect vacuum
/ˈpɜː.fɪkt ˈvæk.juːm/ 38

period /ˈpɪə.ri.əd/ 10

permissible /pəˈmɪs.ə.bl̩/ 7

perpendicular to
/ˌpɜː.pənˈdɪk.jʊl.ə tə/ 5

petrol engine
/ˈpet.rəl ˈen.dʒɪn/ 40

phase /feɪz/ 44, 45

photosensor
/ˌfəʊ.təʊˈsen.sə/ XIII

photovoltaic cell (PV)
/ˌfəʊ.təʊ.vɒlˈteɪ.ik sel/ 44

piercing /ˈpɪə.sɪŋ/ 24

piezoelectric sensor
/pi.et.səʊ.ɪˈlek.trɪk ˈsen.sə/ XIII

pile cap /paɪl kæp/ V

pile /paɪl/ V

pin joint /pɪn dʒɔɪnt/ 32

pinion /ˈpɪn.jən/ 41

pin-jointed /pɪn ˈdʒɔɪn.tɪd/ 32

pipe /paɪp/ 21, 31

pipe fitting /paɪp ˈfɪt.ɪŋ/ 37

pipeline /ˈpaɪp.laɪn/ 37

pipework /ˈpaɪp.wɜːk/ 37

piston /ˈpɪs.tən/ 40

piston cylinder
/ˈpɪs.tən ˈsɪl.ɪn.də/ 40

pitch /pɪtʃ/ 39

pivot (v) /ˈpɪv.ət/ 33

plain washer /pleɪn ˈwɒ.ʃə/ 26

plan /plæn/ 1

plane /pleɪn/ 4

planed /pleɪnd/ 17

plasma /ˈplæz.mə/ 24

plasma cutting
/ˈplæz.mə ˈkʌt.ɪŋ/ 24

plasma torch /ˈplæz.mə tɔːtʃ/ 24

plastic (adj) /ˈplæs.tɪk/ 18

plastic (n) /ˈplæs.tɪk/ 14

plastic deformation
/ˈplæs.tɪk ˌde.fəˈmeɪ.ʃən/ 18

plastically deformed
/ˈplæs.tɪk.li dɪˈfɔːmd/ 18

plasticity /plæsˈtɪ.sə.ti/ 18

plasticizer /ˈplæs.tɪ.saɪz.ə/ 16

plate (v) /pleɪt/ 13

plate /pleɪt/ 21

play (n) /pleɪ/ 7, 25

plug /plʌg/ 27
    as a screw 27
    as a pipe fitting IX
    in electrical appliances 45

plumb /plʌm/ 4

plus /plʌs/ 8

plus or minus /plʌs ə ˈmaɪn.əs/ 7

ply /plaɪ/ 17

plywood /ˈplaɪ.wʊd/ 17

point /pɔɪnt/ 8

point load /pɔɪnt ləʊd/ 30, V

pointed /ˈpɔɪn.tɪd/ 22

polycarbonate
/ˌpɒl.iˈkɑː.bən.eɪt/ 14

polyimide /ˌpɒ.lɪ.əˈmaɪd/ 14

polymer /ˈpɒl.ɪ.mə/ 14

polyvinyl adhesive (PVA)
/ˌpɒl.iˈvaɪnl ədˈhiː.sɪv/ 29

polyvinylchloride (PVC)
/ˌpɒl.i.vaɪn.lˈklɔː.raɪd/ 14

pop rivet /pɒp ˈrɪv.ɪt/ 27

populate (v) /ˈpɒp.jə.leɪt/ 45

port /pɔːt/ 40

positive charge
/ˈpɒz.ə.tɪv tʃɑːdʒ/ 43

positive pressure
/ˈpɒz.ə.tɪv ˈpre.ʃə/ 38

positive terminal
/ˈpɒz.ə.tɪv ˈtɜː.mɪn.əl/ 13

potential energy
/pəˈten.ʃəl ˈen.ə.dʒi/ 35

potentiometer
/pəˌten.ʃiˈɒm.ɪ.tə/ XII

pounds per square inch (psi)
/paʊnz pə skweə rɪnʃ/ 38

pour /pɔː/ 16

powder /ˈpaʊ.də/ 21

power (n) /paʊə/ 35, 43

power (v) /paʊə/ 35, 40

power circuit /paʊə ˈsɜː.kɪt/ 45

power grid /paʊə grɪd/ 44

power hacksaw
/paʊə ˈhæk.sɔː/ 23

power line /paʊə laɪn/ 44

power rating /paʊə ˈreɪt.ɪŋ/ 43

power socket /paʊə ˈsɒk.ɪt/ 45

power station
/paʊə ˈsteɪ.ʃən/ 44

powerful /ˈpaʊə.fəl/ 35

precast (v) /ˌpriːˈkɑːst/ 16

precast concrete
/ˌpriːˈkɑːst ˈkɒŋ.kriːt/ 16

precious metal
/ˈpre.ʃəs ˈmet.l̩/ 13

precipitation hardened
/prɪˌsɪp.ɪˈteɪ.ʃən ˈhɑː.dənd/ 20

precise /prɪˈsaɪs/ 7

precision /prɪˈsɪ.ʒən/ 7

predrilled /priːˈdrɪld/ 27

preliminary drawing
/prɪˈlɪm.ɪn.əri ˈdrɔː.ɪŋ/ 2

preload /ˈpriːləʊd/ 26

pressure /ˈpre.ʃə/ 38

pressure differential
/ˈpre.ʃə ˌdɪf.ɪˈren.ʃl̩/ 38

pressure drag /ˈpre.ʃə dræg/ 39

pressure gauge /ˈpre.ʃə geɪdʒ/ 38

pressure vessel /ˈpre.ʃə ˈves.l̩/ 37

pressurize /ˈpre.ʃə.raɪz/ 38

prestressed /ˌpriːˈstrest/ 16

prestressing /ˌpriːˈstres.ɪŋ/ 16

prime (v) /praɪm/ X

printed circuit
/ˈprɪn.tɪd ˈsɜː.kɪt/ 45

printed circuit board (PCB)
/ˈprɪn.tɪd ˈsɜː.kɪt bɔːd/ 45

profile /ˈprəʊ.faɪl/ 39

propel /prəˈpel/ 39

propeller /prəˈpel.ə/ 39

proportional to
/prəˈpɔː.ʃən.əl tə/ 18, 30

proposed /prəˈpəʊzd/ 3

proud /praʊd/ 22

provide support
/prəˈvaɪd səˈpɔːt/ 25

proximity sensor
/prɒkˈsɪm.ə.ti ˈsen.sə/ XIII

psi (pounds per square inch)
/saɪ/ 38

pulley /ˈpʊl.i/ 42

pulley wheel /ˈpʊl.i wiːl/ 42

pullout force /ˈpʊl.aʊt fɔːs/ 27

pump (n) /pʌmp/ 37

pump (v) /pʌmp/ 37

punch (n) /pʌnʃ/ 24

punched /pʌnʃt/ 24

PV (photovoltaic cell)
/ˌpiːˈviː/ 44

PVA (polyvinyl adhesive)
/ˌpiː.viːˈjeɪ/ 29

PVC (polyvinylchloride)
/ˌpiː.viːˈsiː/ 14

quantify /ˈkwɒn.tɪ.faɪ/ 3

quenched /kwenʃt/ 20

quenching /ˈkwenʃ.ɪŋ/ 20

radiation /ˌreɪ.diˈeɪ.ʃən/ 36

radiator /ˈreɪ.di.eɪ.tə/ 36

radio waves
/ˈreɪ.di.əʊ weɪvz/ VII

radius/radii
/ˈreɪ.di.əs/, /ˈreɪ.di.aɪ/ 6

raft foundation
/rɑːft faʊnˈdeɪ.ʃən/ V

raised /reɪzd/ 22

range /reɪndʒ/ 7

rate (n) /reɪt/ 10

servomechanism
/'sɜː.vəʊˌmek.ən.ɪzm/ 45
set (v) /set/ 14, 16
set in /set ɪn/ 27
set into /set 'ɪn.tə/ 27
set of drawings
/set əv 'drɔː.ɪŋz/ 1
set out /set aʊt/ 5
set screw /set skruː/ 27
seventy-five percent efficient
/'sev.ən.ti faɪv pə'sent ɪ'fɪ.ʃənt/ 35
sewer /'sʊə/ 37
shaft /ʃɑːft/ 26
shaft /ʃɑːft/ 41
shank /ʃæŋk/ 26
shatter /'ʃæ.tə/ 15
shear (n) /ʃɪə/ 31
shear (v) /ʃɪə/ 24, 31
shear force /ʃɪə fɔːs/ 24, 26
shear stress /ʃɪə stres/ 31
shearing /'ʃɪə.rɪŋ/ 31
sheave /ʃiːv/ 42
sheet /ʃiːt/ 15
sheet of metal /ʃiːt əv 'met.l/ 21
shielded metal arc welding (SMAW)
/'ʃiːl.dɪd 'met.l ɑːk 'wel.dɪŋ/ 28
shielding gas /'ʃiːl.dɪŋ gæs/ 28
shift (v) /ʃɪft/ 41
shim /ʃɪm/ 25
shop head /ʃɒp hed/ 27
short circuit /ʃɔːt 'sɜː.kɪt/ 45
shot-peened /'ʃɒt.piːnd/ 20
shot-peening /'ʃɒt.piː.nɪŋ/ 20
shut off /ʃʌt ɒf/ IX
shuttering /'ʃʌt.ə.rɪŋ/ 16
sign off /saɪn ɒf/ 2
signal /'sɪg.nəl/ 2
silica /'sɪl.ɪk.ə/ 15
silicon /'sɪl.ɪ.kn/ 15
silver /'sɪl.və/ 13
simple machine
/'sɪm.pl mə'ʃiːn/ 33
simply supported beam
/'sɪm.pli sə'pɔː.tɪd biːm/ 31
sine wave /saɪn weɪv/ 44
single-phase /'sɪŋ.gl feɪz/ 44
sintered /'sɪnt.əd weɪv/ 20
sintering /'sɪnt.ə.rɪŋ/ 20
siphon (n) /'saɪ.fn/ X
siphon (v) /'saɪ.fn/ X
siphonic action
/saɪ'fɒn.ɪk 'æk.ʃn/ 38, X

siphonic drainage
/saɪ'fɒn.ɪk 'dreɪ.nɪdʒ/ X
size (v) /saɪz/ 3
sketch /sketʃ/ 2
skin friction /skɪn 'frɪk.ʃən/ 39
slab /slæb/ V
slipstream /'slɪp.striːm/ 39
slot head screw
/slɒt hed skruː/ 27
slot into /slɒt 'ɪn.tə/ 22
slot through /slɒt θruː/ 25
small scale /smɔːl skeɪl/ 1
small-section /smɔːl 'sek.ʃn/ 9
SMAW (shielded metal arc welding) /smɔː/ 28
smoke detector
/sməʊk dɪ'tek.tə/ XIII
socket /'sɒk.ɪt/ 45, IX
socket head /'sɒk.ɪt hed/ 26
soft /sɒft/ 19
soft soldering
/sɒft 'səʊl.də.rɪŋ/ 29
softwood /'sɒf.wʊd/ 17
solder /'səʊl.də/ 29
soldered /'səʊl.dəd/ 29
soldering /'səʊl.də.rɪŋ/ 29
soldering iron
/'səʊl.də.rɪŋ aɪ.ən/ 29
solid rivet /'sɒl.ɪd 'rɪv.ɪt/ 27
solid wire /'sɒl.ɪd waɪə/ 21
solid wood /'sɒl.ɪd wʊd/ 17
solidify /sə'lɪ.dɪ.faɪ/ 36
solvent /'sɒl.vənt/ 29
sound energy /saʊnd 'en.ə.dʒi/ 2
spacer /'speɪ.sə/ 25
span (n) /spæn/ 4
span (v) /spæn/ 4
spanner /'spæn.ə/ 26
spare capacity
/speə kə'pæ.sə.ti/ 10
spark erosion
/spɑːk ɪ'rəʊ.ʒən/ 24
spark plug /spɑːk plʌg/ 40
speaker/loudspeaker
/'spiː.kə ˌlaʊd'spiː.kə/ XII
specific heat capacity
/spə'sɪ.fɪk hiːt kə'pæ.sə.ti/ 36
specification /ˌspes.ɪ.fɪ'keɪ.ʃən/ 3
specify /'spes.ɪ.faɪ/ 3
specimen /'spes.ə.mɪn/ 30
spot welding /spɒt 'wel.dɪŋ/ 29
spread the load
/spred ðə ləʊd/ 26
spring washer /sprɪŋ 'wɒ.ʃə/ 26

sprocket /'sprɒk.ɪt/ 42
spur gear /spɜː gɪə/ 41
square (v) /skweə/ 8
square (n) /skweə/ 22
square bar /skweə bɑː/ 21
square millimetre (mm²)
/skweə 'mɪl.ɪˌmiː.tə/ 9
square off (v) /skweə rɒf/ 5
square tube /skweə tjuːb/ 21
stainless steel /'steɪn.ləs stiːl/ 12
state /steɪt/ 36
static friction
/'stæ.tɪk 'frɪk.ʃən/ 34
static load /'stæ.tɪk ləʊd/ V
statically determinate structure /'stæ.tɪk.li dɪ'tɜː.mɪn.ət 'strʌk.tʃə/ 32
steam /stiːm/ VII
steel /stiːl/ 12
step down /step daʊn/ 44
step up /step ʌp/ 44
step-down transformer
/step daʊn træns'fɔːm.ə/ 44
step-up transformer
/step ʌp træns'fɔːm.ə/ 44
stick welding /stɪk 'wel.dɪŋ/ 28
stiction /'stɪk.ʃən/ 34
stiff /stɪf/ 18, 32
stiffen /'stɪf.ən/ 32
store (v) /stɔː/ 35
strain /streɪn/ 30
strain energy
/streɪn 'en.ə.dʒi/ 35
strained /streɪnd/ 30
strand /strænd/ 21
stranded wire
/'stræn.dɪd waɪə/ 21
streamlined /'striːm.laɪnd/ 39
stress /stres/ 30
stress grade /stres greɪd/ 17
stressed /strest/ 30
stress-graded /stres 'greɪd.ɪd/ 17
strike (v) /straɪk/ 4
strike an electric arc
/straɪk ən ɪ'lek.trɪk ɑːk/ 28
strip foundation
/strɪp faʊn'deɪ.ʃən/ V
stroke /strəʊk/ 40
structural member
/'strʌk.tʃə.rəl 'mem.bə/ 31, 32
structural steel section
/'strʌk.tʃə.rəl stiːl 'sek.ʃn/ 21
structural strength
/'strʌk.tʃə.rəl streŋθ/ 16

under hydrostatic pressure /'ʌn.də ˌhaɪ.drə'stæt.ɪk 'pre.ʃə/ 38

under pressure /'ʌn.də 'pre.ʃə/ 38

uniformly distributed load (UDL) /'juː.nɪ.fɔːm.li dɪ'strɪb.juː.tɪd ləʊd/ 30, V

union /'juː.ni.ən/ IX

universal beam (UB) /ˌjuː.nɪ'vɜː.səl biːm/ V

universal column (UC) /ˌjuː.nɪ'vɜː.səl 'kɒl.əm/ V

universal joint /juː.nɪ'vɜː.səl dʒɔɪnt/ XI

unscrew /ʌn'skruː/ 26

upstream of /ʌp'striːm əv/ 39

useful energy /'juːs.fəl 'en.ə.dʒi/ 35

UTS (ultimate tensile strength) /ˌjuː.ti'ti'jes/ 18

vacuum /'væk.juːm/ 38

valve /vælv/ 37, IX

vanadium /və'neɪ.di.əm/ 12

vaporize /'veɪ.pə.raɪz/ 36

vapour /'veɪ.pə/ 36, VII

variation /ˌveə.ri'eɪ.ʃən/ 7

vary /'veə.ri/ 7

vector /'vek.tə/ 30

vector quantity /'vek.tə 'kwɒn.tə.ti/ 30

velocity /vɪ'lɒs.ə.ti/ 33

vertical plane /'vɜː.tɪ.kl pleɪn/ 4

vessel /'ves.l/ 37

view /vjuː/ 1

visually stress-graded /'vɪʒ.u.ə.li stres 'greɪd.ɪd/ 17

vitrified /'vɪt.rɪ.faɪd/ 15

void /vɔɪd/ 22

volt (V) /vəʊlt/ 43

voltage /'vəʊl.tɪdʒ/ 43

voltmeter /'vəʊlt,miː.tə/ XIII

volume /'vɒl.juːm/ 9

vortex/vortices /'vɔː.teks/, /'vɔː.tɪ.siːz/ 39

W (watt) /wɒt/ 35, 43

wafer /'weɪf.ə/ 45

waist /weɪst/ 18

wake /weɪk/ 39

wall plug /wɔːl plʌg/ 27

washer /'wɒʃ.ə/ 26

waste energy /weɪst 'en.ə.dʒi/ 35

water main /'wɔː.tə meɪn/ 37

water vapour /'wɔː.tə 'veɪ.pə/ 36, VII

water–cement ratio /ˌwɔː.tə.sɪ'ment 'reɪ.ʃi.əʊ/ 16

watertight /'wɔː.tə.taɪt/ 37

watt (W) /wɒt/ 35, 43

wattage /'wɒt.ɪdʒ/ 43

wattmeter /'wɒt,miː.tə/ XIII

watts /wɒts/ 40

wear (n) /weə/ 19

weigh /weɪ/ 9

weight /weɪt/ 9

weightless /'weɪt.ləs/ 9

weld (n) /weld/ 28

weld pool /weld puːl/ 28

weld to (v) /weld tə/ 28

weld together /weld tə'ge.ðə/ 28

weld zone /weld zəʊn/ 28

welded /'wel.dɪd/ 28

welding rod /'wel.dɪŋ rɒd/ 28

white hot /waɪt hɒt/ 20

whole number /həʊl 'nʌm.bə/ 8

width /wɪtθ/ 4

wind tunnel /wɪnd 'tʌn.əl/ 39

wind turbine /wɪnd 'tɜː.baɪn/ 37

windscreen (BrE) /'wɪn.skriːn/ / windshield (AmE) /'wɪn.ʃiːld/ 15

wing /wɪŋ/ 39

wire /waɪə/ 21

wire rope /waɪə rəʊp/ 42

within tolerance /wɪ'ðɪn 'tɒl.ə.rəns/ 7

work (n) /wɜːk/ 35

work done /wɜːk dʌn/ 35

work harden (v) /wɜːk 'hɑː.dn/ 20

work hardened /wɜːk 'hɑː.dənd/ 20

work loose /wɜːk luːs/ 26

work to /wɜːk tə/ 2

working drawing /'wɜː.kɪŋ 'drɔː.ɪŋ/ 2

working metal /'wɜː.kɪŋ 'met.l/ 20

workpiece /'wɜː.k,piːs/ 23

worm /wɜːm/ 41

worm gear /wɜːm gɪə/ 41

worst-case scenario /'wɜːs.keɪs sɪ'nɑː.ri.əʊ/ 3

XNOR gate /'eks.nɔː geɪt/ XII

XOR gate /'ek.sɔː geɪt/ XII

x-rays /'eks.reɪz/ VII

yield (v) /jiːld/ 18

yield point /jiːld pɔɪnt/ 18

zero /'zɪə.rəʊ/ 8

zinc /zɪŋk/ 13

Acknowledgements

I'd like to thank the following people for their contribution to *Professional English in Use Engineering:* Lyn Strutt, whose considerable expertise and energy have helped to shape every aspect of the book; Clare Sheridan for getting the project off the ground and for her helpful guidance during the early stages; Caroline Thiriau and Nik White for their valuable editorial input; Colin Hobart for casting his expert eye over the manuscripts and for his helpful suggestions; Nick Robinson for sharing his knowledge of ESP; and Veena Holkar for successfully handling the tricky task of photo research.

And special thanks to Nathalie, Aimy and Tom (born between Units 23 and 24) for putting up with me during a very busy year.

Mark Ibbotson August 2009

/ jocicalek p. 40 (br); Shutterstock / Joe Gough p. 49 (photo 3); Shutterstock / Kondrachov Vladimir p. 58 (bu) p. 58 (bl); Shutterstock / Konjushenko Vladimir Iljich p. 60 (bc); Shutterstock / Les Scholz p.74; Shutterstock / Lora Clark p. 49 (photo 8); Shutterstock / Maksim Toome p. 43; Shutterstock / martin florek p. 97 (l); Shutterstock / Masterov Egor p. 65; Shutterstock / Michael Shake p. 85; Shutterstock / Mircea BERZERGHEANU p. 49 (photo 2), p. 49 (photo 4); Shutterstock / Mona Makela p. 53 (photo 1); Shutterstock / mumbo jumbo p. 15; Shutterstock / Nicola Gavin p. 21; Shutterstock / Nicole Gordine p. 62 (b); Shutterstock / Orange Line Media p. 38 (r); Shutterstock / Orla p. 19; Shutterstock / PeppPic p. 57 (tr); Shutterstock / R. Gino Santa Maria p. 53 (photo 4); Shutterstock / Ricardo A. Alves p. 57 (tc); Shutterstock / Richard Williamson p. 60 (tfr); Shutterstock / Slavoljub Pantelic p. 72, p. 91; Shutterstock / Steve Snowden p. 40 (bc); Shutterstock / Taiga p. 40 (t); Shutterstock / Tatiana Popova p. 80 (r); Shutterstock / Trombax p. 64; Shutterstock / Vakhrushev Pavel p. 26 (b); Shutterstock / Val Thoermer p. 19; Shutterstock / YellowCrest Media p. 86; Shutterstock / Yury Kosourov p. 48 (l), p. 49 (photo 10), p. 76; Shutterstock / yuyangc p. 113; Shutterstock/ fatbob p. 49 (photo 12);

Illustrations:

Ron Dixon and Kamae Design

The publishers are grateful to the following contributors:

Editor: Lyn Strutt
Reviewers: Colin Hobart, Kevin Westbrook
Designer: Stephanie White
Proofreader: Marcus Fletcher
Picture researcher: Veena Holkar

Cover design by David Lawton at Cambridge University Press

Designed and typeset by Kamae Design, Oxford, UK